American Book Company
The Standards Experts

Y0-CBL-966

MASTERING THE GEORGIA 7TH GRADE CRCT IN SOCIAL STUDIES

AFRICA AND ASIA

Developed to the New Georgia Performance Standards
Revised – October 2009

Kindred Howard

Andrew Cox
Joshua Williams
Mark J. Fleszar
Lisa Bryde
Gerald Shoats

Special Consultants:

Dr. Mohammed Hassen Ali
Dr. Isa Blumi
Dr. Douglas Reynolds

American Book Company
PO Box 2638
Woodstock, GA 30188-1383
Toll Free: 1 (888) 264-5877   Phone: (770) 928-2834
Fax: (770) 928-7483   Toll Free Fax: 1 (866) 827-3240
www.americanbookcompany.com

ACKNOWLEDGEMENTS

The authors would like to gratefully acknowledge the formatting and technical contributions of Marsha Torrens and Becky Wright.

We also want to thank Mary Stoddard for developing the graphics for this book.

This product/publication includes images from CorelDRAW 9 and 11 which are protected by the copyright laws of the United States, Canada, and elsewhere. Used under license.

Chapter 2: Historical Understandings of Africa   35

Chapter 3: Political and Economic Understandings of Africa   43

Chapter 5: Historical Understandings of Southwest Asia   79

Chapter 6: Political and Economic Understandings of Southwest Asia   93

Chapter 7: Geographic Understandings of Southern and Eastern Asia   101

Chapter 8: Historical Understandings of Southern and Eastern Asia   119

PREFACE

Mastering the 7th Grade CRCT in Social Studies: Africa and Asia will help students who are learning or reviewing material for the CRCT. The materials in this book are based on the testing standards as published by the Georgia Department of Education. This book is written to the grade 7 social studies level and corresponds to 950 to 1075L on the Lexile text measure scale.

This book contains several sections. These sections are as follows: 1) general information about the book; 2) a diagnostic test; 3) an evaluation chart; 4) chapters that teach the concepts and skills that improve graduation readiness; 5) two practice tests. Answers to the tests and exercises are in a separate manual. The answer manual also contains a Chart of Standards for teachers to make a more precise diagnosis of student needs and assignments.

We welcome comments and suggestions about the book. Please contact the author at

American Book Company
PO Box 2638
Woodstock, GA 30188-1383

Toll Free: 1 (888) 264-5877
Phone: (770) 928-2834
Fax: (770) 928-7483
Web site: www.americanbookcompany.com

ABOUT THE AUTHORS

Lead Author:

Kindred Howard is a 1991 alumnus of the University of North Carolina at Chapel Hill, where he graduated with a B.S. in criminal justice and national honors in political science. In addition to two years as a probation and parole officer in North Carolina, he has served for over twelve years as a teacher and writer in the fields of religion and social studies. His experience includes teaching students at both the college and high school level, as well as speaking at numerous seminars and authoring several books on U.S. history, American government, and economics. Mr. Howard is currently completing a M.A. in history from Georgia State University. In addition to serving as Social Studies Coordinator for American Book Company, Mr. Howard is the president/CEO of KB Howard Freelance Writing and lives in Powder Springs, Georgia, with his wife and three children.

Andrew Cox graduated with honors from Kennesaw State University in 2007, where he studied international affairs, focusing on the political and economic development of Asia and post-communist Europe.

Joshua Williams is a 2006 alumnus of Georgia State University where he graduated *magna cum laude* with a B.A. in history and a minor in political science. He is currently completing a M.A. in social studies at Georgia State University.

Mark J. Fleszar is a May 2008 graduate of the Master's Program in World and Atlantic History at Georgia State University. Mr. Fleszar begins his doctoral training in history this fall.

Lisa Bryde is a 1986 graduate of Georgia State University where she graduated with a B.S. in Secondary English Education. She completed her M.A. in curriculum development and design at the University of Georgia, where she is currently completing her doctorate in curriculum development as well. In addition to her fourteen years as a language arts teacher and writer in various fields of curriculum, Ms Bryde is also an advocate and speaker for Brain Based Learning. She currently serves as Director of Curriculum for one of the largest distance learning companies in the United States and, lives in Lawrenceville, Georgia, with her husband, daughter, and four dogs.

ABOUT THE SPECIAL CONSULTANTS

Dr. Mohammed Hassen Ali is a professor of history at Georgia State University. His area of expertise is African history, politics, and culture.

Dr. Isa Blumi is a professor of history at Georgia State University. His area of expertise is Southwest Asian history, politics, and culture, with specialization in the history and culture of the Ottoman Empire.

Dr. Douglas Reynolds is a professor of history at Georgia State University. His area of expertise is Southern and Eastern Asian history, politics, and culture.

Georgia CRCT in SS: Africa and Asia Diagnostic Test

The purpose of this diagnostic test is to measure your knowledge in social studies. This test is based on the GPS-based Georgia CRCT in Social Studies and adheres to the sample question format provided by the Georgia Department of Education.

General Directions:

1. Read all directions carefully.

2. Read each question or sample. Then choose the best answer.

3. Choose only one answer for each question. If you change an answer, be sure to erase your original answer completely.

4. After taking the test, you or your instructor should score it using the evaluation chart following the test. Circle any questions you did not get correct and review those chapters.

1. The Ottomans were a powerful   SS7H2
    CH 5

    A   Muslim empire.

    B   Christian empire.

    C   Colonial empire.

    D   West African empire.

2. Which statement below is   SS7CG1
    most accurate in describing   SS7CG4
    SS7CG6
    an autocratic   CH 3, 6, 9
    government?

    A   The people elect the president to a
        five-year term.

    B   The three levels of government are
        national, provincial, and local.

    C   The parliament seeks to control the
        way citizens think.

    D   What the leader says, goes.

3. What are three basic   SS7E1
    economic questions?   SS7E5
    SS7E8
    CH 3, 6, 9
    A   Where to produce? Why
        produce? For whom to
        produce?

    B   What to produce? How to
        Produce? For whom to produce?

    C   Where to produce? How to
        produce? Why produce?

    D   What to produce? How to produce?
        Why produce?

4. Which ethnic group lacks its   SS7G8
    own country, lives in Turkey   CH 4
    and Iraq, and is often subject to
    discrimination?

    A   Bedouins   C   Kurds

    B   Druze   D   Berbers

Read the list below, and answer the following question.

- series of islands
- large Muslim population
- president is most powerful figure in the government
- depends on rubber as an important natural resource
- home to groups like the Papuans

5. What country is the above list   SS7G9
    referring to?   CH 7

    A   India   C   Vietnam

    B   Indonesia   D   Japan

6. Which of the following two   SS7H3
    countries benefited the **most**   CH 8
    from U.S. economic help after WWII?

    A   China and Japan

    B   Japan and North Korea

    C   Japan and South Korea

    D   China and North Korea

7. The first people to enslave   SS7H1
    Africans were   CH 2

    A   black Africans.

    B   white Europeans.

    C   Indian immigrants.

    D   Afrikaners in South Africa.

8. During the rainy season,   SS7G10
    villages along the Yangtze and   CH 7
    Ganges rivers have to worry about

    A   desalinization.

    B   flooding.

    C   deforestation.

    D   urbanization.

Look at the map below, and answer the following question.

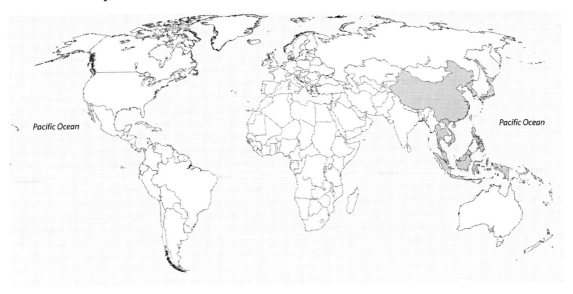

Pacific Ocean

Pacific Ocean

9. This shaded areas on the map above depict

    A Southwest Asia.

    B Arabia.

    C Eastern Asia.

    D Africa.

10. Haymonot's family once farmed the regions south of his village. However, poor farming methods and years of famine have left the land dry and unable to be used for agriculture. It sounds like the area has fallen victim to

    A deforestation.

    B desalinization.

    C desertification.

    D Buddhism.

11. Muhammad was a prophet who preached that there is only one God. Many powerful leaders rejected this prophet, thinking he was a threat to their economic security. Muhammad fled his hometown and settled in Mecca. His enemies followed him, but they were defeated by Muhammad and his forces. He soon converted most of Arabia to the religion of

    A Judaism.

    B Christianity.

    C Buddhism.

    D Islam.

12. What is OPEC? SS7E6 CH 6

A a group of oil-producing countries that work together to look after their economic interests

B a group of government officials who regulates the amount of petroleum Saudi Arabia can export

C an organization devoted to helping countries outside of the Middle East export oil

D a group of officials that decides which Middle Eastern countries are allowed to import oil

13. How did African nationalists feel about the partitioning of Africa to European powers? SS7H1 CH 2

A They were supportive because they valued Europeans as allies.

B They were grateful because it increased economic development.

C They did not care because they had no idea what was happening in Europe.

D They were resentful and wanted to establish independent African nations.

14. Which country is the following list referring to? SS7CG4 SS7CG5 CH 6

- has a parliamentary and representative democracy
- consists of popularly elected officials who enact laws and regulate government activity
- has an independent judicial branch made up of religious and non religious courts
- has the most developed economy in Southwest Asia

A Israel

B Saudi Arabia

C Iran

D Kenya

15. Increased industrialization in India and China leads to SS7G10 CH 7

A more air pollution.

B desertification.

C less currency.

D less economic development.

16. In order to have a good budget, you need to make sure that SS7E4 CH 10

A you have a lot of debt.

B your income is more than your expenses.

C your expenses are greater than your income.

D you have credit.

17. Where would one expect to find the **most** people? SS7G9 SS7G11 CH 7

A Beijing, China

B the upper Himalayas

C the Gobi Desert

D Congo Rainforest

Read the quote below, and answer the following question.

> "It is like the 'Black Death' of our generation; a plague upon Africa. It kills mothers, fathers, and children. Roughly a third of its victims are in Africa. The world must respond. Until we overcome this killer, it will continue to ravish Africa and, eventually, the world. I call on nations of the developed world to devote whatever resources are necessary to finding a cure. I call on you to declare war!"

18. The speaker is **most** likely SS7CG2 CH 3

A angry about apartheid.

B a Palestinian preaching against Israel.

C trying to raise more money for AIDS research.

D pleading for relief from famines.

19. Why is the Sahara Desert considered a trade barrier? SS7E2 CH 3

A because it encourages foreigners to sneak into Africa for illegal trading

B because it makes trade more difficult in Africa

C because it is easy to travel through

D because it increases the chances of trading with poor countries

20. Why did the United States invade Afghanistan in 2001? SS7H2 CH 5

A After the 9/11 attacks, the United States vowed that it would go after foreign terrorists rather than waiting for them to attack again.

B After the 9/11 attacks, the U.S. government decided to flee to Afghanistan and hide from bin Laden

C The United States wanted to attack Muslim terrorists in response to the Gulf War of 1990.

D The United States claimed that Afghanistan belonged to it as a result of the cold war.

21. What is a market economy? SS7E1 SS7E5 SS7E8 CH 3, 6, 9

A The government regulates most of the economy.

B The government has little regulation and allows for private ownership of business and property.

C The king or queen has complete control.

D Most businesses and property belong to the state, rather than private businesses or individuals.

22. How does drilling for oil hurt the environment? SS7G2 SS7G6 CH 1, 4

A The drilling releases desertification.

B The methods of oil extraction leave the land damaged and unusable.

C The drilling creates unsafe working environments.

D The machines used for extraction decrease nations' populations.

Look at the map below, and answer the following question.

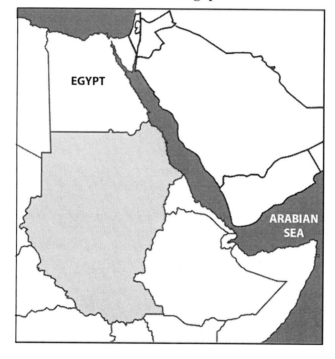

23. The shaded area on the map above depicts

    A Israel.

    B South Africa.

    C India.

    D Sudan.

SS7G1
CH 1

24. **Most** people who live in the Sahel or Sahara are nomadic. Why do people who live in these regions need to move from place to place?

SS7G1
SS7G4
CH 1

    A because they are in search of better climates as the seasons change

    B in order to search for oil to export

    C because they must constantly find water and grazing areas

    D in order to escape industrial pollution

25. How does oil, a natural resource, affect the economic development of Africa?

SS7E3
CH 3

    A Because it is the only natural resource in Africa, nations do not profit from oil.

    B Almost all nations in Africa depend on agriculture, not oil, for revenue.

    C Foreign investors buy all the oil so Africa does not profit.

    D African nations rich in oil will export large amounts of it, producing lots of revenue.

26. Which of the following describes India's government? SS7CG7 CH 9

   A   federal republic with an elected parliament and twenty-eight states

   B   one-party system with a unicameral legislature

   C   democracy with a president as the most powerful figure

   D   constitutional monarchy, in which the prime minister has most of the power

27. Someone wanting to live in an Eastern Asian country with free markets, lots of economic development, and a culture similar to the West, would probably be **most** at home in which two countries? SS7E8 SS7H3 CH 8, 9

   A   North Korea and China

   B   China and Japan

   C   North Korea and South Korea

   D   South Korea and Japan

28. Chinese factories, heavy machinery, and construction of new industrial centers in Indonesia are all examples of SS7E3 SS7E7 SS7E10 CH 3, 6, 9

   A   investments in capital goods.

   B   state-owned businesses.

   C   efforts to improve literacy.

   D   investments in human capital.

29. Hinduism began in SS7H3 SS7G12 CH 7, 8

   A   Africa.

   B   Turkey.

   C   India.

   D   China.

30. In recent decades, India has moved from a command economy towards a market economy in order to SS7E8 CH 9

   A   slow economic development.

   B   give the government greater economic control.

   C   increase revenue and improve the quality of life in India.

   D   end its one-party rule.

31. Why does Africa owe its independence largely to literacy and education? SS7G4 SS7H1 CH 1, 2

   A   The nationalist movement encouraged uneducated blacks to learn to read and write.

   B   Many of the nationalist movements were led by educated blacks.

   C   Since much of Africa's population is illiterate, they fought for their independence in order to improve the literacy rate of the people.

   D   Only literate blacks were granted their independence.

32. What is the **most** important factor in determining what a country produces, exports, and imports? SS7E3 SS7E7 SS7E10 CH 3, 6, 9

   A   the amount of debt the country is in

   B   the amount of people who live in the country

   C   the government's policies on foreign investments

   D   a country's location and available natural resources

Look at the map below, and answer the following question.

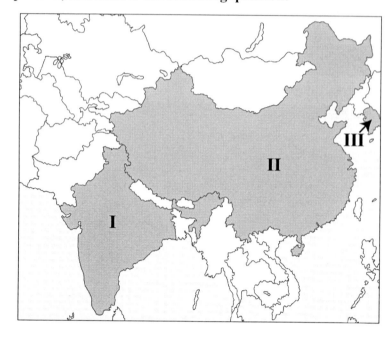

33. In which area would one find the **most** Hindus?

SS7G9
SS7G12
CH 7

    A I

    B II

    C III

    D Hinduism is not practiced in any of these areas.

34. Why does Egypt face problems with air pollution?

SS7G2
CH 1

    A The Aswan Dam contributes greatly to air pollution by interfering with the Nile River.

    B Cigarette smoke, cleaning fluids, and building materials pollute the air.

    C Large populations, factories, and traffic contaminate the air.

    D Much of Asia's air pollution is in Egypt.

35. If a nation invests money and time into providing training and education for its citizens, what is this an example of?

SS7E3
SS7E7
SS7E10
CH 3, 6, 9

    A investment in entrepreneurship

    B investment in capital goods

    C investment in tariff

    D investment in human capital

Look at the map below, and answer the following question.

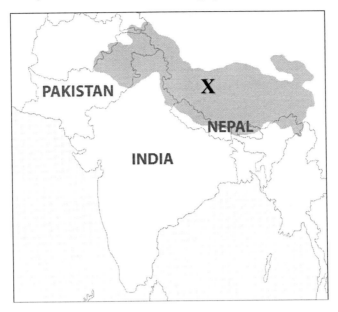

36. What label should be placed where the X is? SS7G9
CH 7

   A Himalayan Mountains

   B Sahara Desert

   C Gobi Desert

   D the Sahel

37. What is the human-made waterway that connects the Mediterranean Sea and the Red Sea? SS7G5
CH 4

   A Suez Canal

   B Strait of Hormuz

   C Gaza Strip

   D Persian Gulf

38. Retirement, health care, college, and vacations are all SS7E4
CH 10

   A examples of economic growth.

   B caused by debt.

   C reasons to save.

   D bad economic choices.

39. What approach did the United States and its allies take to rebuilding Japan after WWII? SS7H3
CH 8

   A They left Japan to rebuild itself.

   B They oversaw the country until it had a stable government and capitalist economy.

   C They established a command economy to be ruled by a military dictator.

   D They did away with the emperor and put a president in charge.

40. Why does economic or political instability in Southwest Asia affect nations worldwide? `SS7E6 CH 6`

A because nations around the globe get most of their agricultural products from Southwest Asia

B because Southwest Asia exports a large percentage of the world's oil and nations around the globe depend on these exports

C because political leaders in Southwest Asia refuse to trade when they are unstable

D because it encourages discontent among civilians and creates conflict in all nations of the world

41. Sudan's government is **best** described as `SS7CG1 CH 3`

A autocratic.

B democratic.

C parliamentary.

D a confederation.

42. India's government is **best** described as a/an `SS7CG6 CH 9`

A communist state.

B confederation.

C oligarchy.

D federation.

43. Efforts to improve the health care of Indians is an example of a/an `SS7E3 SS7E7 SS7E10 CH 3, 6, 9`

A investment in capital goods.

B market economy.

C literacy rate.

D investment in human capital.

44. If someone were lost in the Congo Rainforest, they would be lost in the middle of `SS7G1 CH 1`

A the Sahara.

B Africa.

C the Bay of Bengal.

D China.

45. What is anti-Semitism? `SS7H2 CH 5`

A hatred of Kurdish people

B racism against Muslims

C racism against Jewish people

D hatred of Christians

46. What country is home to the sacred city of Jerusalem? `SS7G5 CH 4`

A Jordan   C Saudi Arabia

B Israel   D Iraq

47. A country ruled by a national government that does not share power with any other level of government operates as a/an `SS7CG1 SS7CG4 SS7CG6 CHS 3, 6, 9`

A confederation.

B federation.

C unitary government.

D autocratic democracy.

48. Millions of people dying of starvation is a tragic consequence of `SS7CG3 CH 3`

A Pan-Africanism.

B the Arab-Israeli conflict.

C economic development.

D famines.

Look at the map below, and answer the following question.

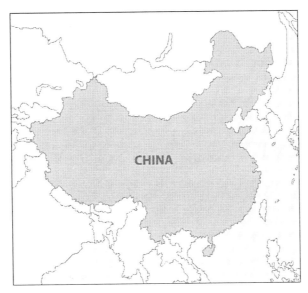

49. The economy of the nation pictured above has traditionally leaned toward being a

    SS7E8
    CH 9

    A   market economy.

    B   capitalist economy.

    C   parliamentary democracy.

    D   command economy.

50. In what economic system does the government own the means of production?

    SS7E1
    SS7E5
    SS7E8
    CH 3, 6, 9

    A   traditional economies

    B   command economies

    C   mixed economies

    D   market economies

51. Which country has the **most** developed economy in Southwest Asia?

    SS7E5
    CH 6

    A   Israel

    B   Saudi Arabia

    C   Iran

    D   Iraq

52. Who believes that only blood relatives of the prophet Muhammed have a right to lead Islam?

    SS7G8
    CH 4

    A   Sunni Muslims

    B   Zionists

    C   Shia Muslims

    D   Hindus

53. When crops fail and there is not enough food, the poor in Africa often suffer from the effects of

    SS7 CG3
    CH 3

    A   AIDS.

    B   flooding.

    C   famine.

    D   industrialization.

54. Mr. Pak has a small business in South Korea. He wants to ship some of his products to India. The buyer in India offers to buy Mr. Wang's product using Indian currency. Before Mr. Wang can know if he is willing to sell for the offered price, he needs to know the

    SS7E2
    SS7E6
    SS7E9
    CH 3, 6, 9

    A natural trade barriers.

    B literacy rate in India.

    C literacy rate in South Korea.

    D exchange rate.

55. What type of government is found in Israel?

    SS7CG5
    CH 6

    A a presidential democracy

    B a constitutional monarchy

    C a parliamentary democracy

    D an absolute monarchy

56. The Communist Party holds power over every aspect of the government in

    SS7CG7
    CH 9

    A South Korea.

    B Japan.

    C Egypt.

    D China.

57. Members of the Knesset and the Diet serve in

    SS7CG5
    CH 6

    A autocratic governments.

    B parliamentary democracies.

    C China's Communist Party.

    D Saudi Arabia's absolute monarchy.

58. Which of the following has helped Japan become the most economically developed nation in Asia?

    SS7E9
    CH 9

    A trade

    B the Cultural Revolution

    C command economies

    D Buddhism

59. When China attempts to restrict U.S. products sold in its country, it is imposing

    SS7E2
    SS7E6
    SS7E9
    CH 3, 6, 9

    A natural trade barriers.

    B political trade barriers.

    C command economies.

    D free trade.

60. Specialization benefits both buyers and sellers because it

    SS7E2
    SS7E6
    SS7E9
    CH 3, 6, 9

    A gets rid of trade barriers.

    B prevents the buyer from having to exchange currency in order to buy what is sold.

    C provides the seller with revenue while providing the buyer with a needed import.

    D prevents free trade and increases tariffs.

Use the map below to answer question 61.

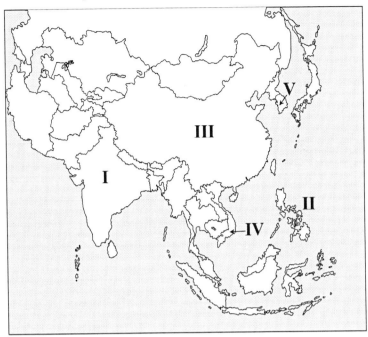

61. Mohandas Gandhi's efforts led to the independence of which area? SS7H3
CH 8

   A I   B IV   C III   D II

62. Which is **true** regarding environmental policies in Southwest Asia? SS7E7
CH 6

  A Policies restricting how resources are extracted can hurt nations that rely on these resources for revenue.

  B The interests of all nations are the same, so governments try to make all policies identical.

  C Governments do not have to be sensitive to economic concerns.

  D Too little regulation can slow economic development.

63. In which nation would a citizen have the **most** say in who runs their government? SS7CG2
CH 3

  A Sudan

  B North Korea

  C South Africa

  D Saudi Arabia

"South Africa sits at the southernmost tip of Africa. For centuries, South Africa has served as a midway point between important trade routes. These trade routes allowed many Europeans to bring capitalism and investors into the region in the late nineteenth century. It is now a highly industrialized and modern country. In fact, it is the most economically developed nation in Africa."

64. After reading this passage, what contributed **most** to South Africa's development as a strong nation?   SS7G3 SS7H1 CH 1, 2

    A   military conquests

    B   the discovery of natural resources

    C   its location

    D   slavery

65. Which of the following nations has a government that is **best** described as a theocracy?   SS7CG5 CH 6

    A   Sudan

    B   Iraq

    C   Iran

    D   Japan

66. Which of the following coun-tries' government **most** resembles a parliamentary democracy?   SS7CG2 CH 3

    A   China

    B   Sudan

    C   Kenya

    D   South Africa

67. Civil wars in Africa leave a country devastated. People flee the country to escape war. What are these people called?   SS7CG3 CH 3

    A   refugees

    B   cowards

    C   prisoners of war

    D   nomads

68. The photo above **most likely** depicts   SS7G10 CH 7

    A   deforestation in Sudan.

    B   extraction in Saudi Arabia.

    C   flooding along the Yangtze.

    D   desertification in Kenya.

Look at the map below, and answer the following question.

69. What industry do the shaded regions **most** rely on?

SS7G7, SS7E7
CH 4, 6

  A agriculture   B oil   C fishing   D military exports

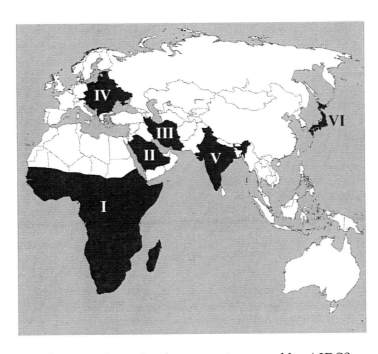

70. Which region on the map above has been **most** ravaged by AIDS?

SS7CG3
CH 3

  A I   B V   C VI   D III

EVALUATION CHART FOR GEORGIA 7TH GRADE CRCT IN SOCIAL STUDIES AFRICA AND ASIA DIAGNOSTIC TEST

Directions: On the following chart, circle the question numbers that you answered incorrectly, and evaluate the results. These questions are based on the *standards and benchmarks published by the Georgia Department of Education.* Then turn to the appropriate chapters, read the explanations, and complete the exercises. Review other chapters as needed. Finally, complete the Practice Test(s) to assess your progress and further prepare you for the **Georgia 7th Grade CRCT**.

Note: Some question numbers may appear under multiple chapters because those questions require demonstration of multiple skills.

Chapter	Diagnostic Test Question(s)
Chapter 1: Geographic Understandings of Africa	10, 22, 23, 24, 31, 34, 44, 64
Chapter 2: Historical Understandings of Africa	7, 13, 31, 64
Chapter 3: Political and Economic Understandings of Africa	2, 3, 18, 19, 21, 25, 28, 32, 35, 41, 43, 47, 48, 50, 53, 54, 59, 60, 63, 66, 67, 70
Chapter 4: Geographic Understandings of Southwest Asia	4, 11, 22, 37, 46, 52, 69
Chapter 5: Historical Understandings of Southwest Asia	1, 11, 20, 45
Chapter 6: Political and Economic Understandings of Southwest Asia	2, 3, 12, 14, 21, 28, 32, 35, 40, 43, 47, 50, 51, 54, 55, 57, 59, 60, 62, 65, 69
Chapter 7: Geographic Understandings of Southern and Eastern Asia	5, 8, 9, 15, 17, 29, 33, 36, 68
Chapter 8: Historical Understandings of Southern and Eastern Asia	6, 27, 29, 39, 61
Chapter 9: Political and Economic Understandings of Southern and Eastern Asia	2, 3, 21, 26, 27, 28, 30, 32, 35, 42, 43, 47, 49, 50, 56, 58, 59, 60
Chapter 10: Personal Money-management Choices	16, 38

Chapter 1
Geographic Understandings of Africa

This chapter covers the following Georgia standards.

SS7G1	The student will locate selected features of Africa.
SS7G2	The student will discuss environmental issues across the continent of Africa.
SS7G3	The student will explain the impact of location, climate, and physical characteristics on population distribution in Africa.
SS7G4	The student will describe the diverse cultures of the people who live in Africa.

1.1 PHYSICAL FEATURES AND NATIONS OF AFRICA

GEOGRAPHIC REGIONS

THE SAHARA DESERT

Geography is the study of the earth's surface. Land, bodies of water, climate, peoples, and natural resources are aspects of geography.

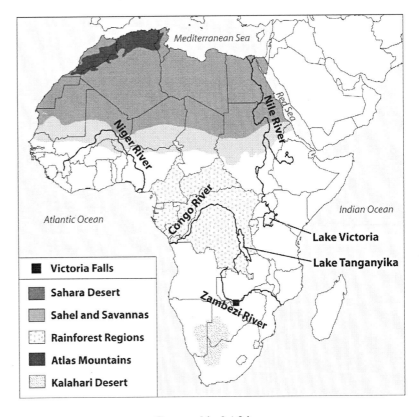

Geographical Africa

Key physical features are part of Africa's geography. **Deserts** are areas that typically get fewer than ten inches of rainfall a year. The **Sahara Desert** stretches across North Africa from the Atlantic Ocean to the Red Sea. The Sahara covers almost one-third of the continent and is the largest desert in the world.

The Sahara Desert is extremely hot and dry. It is hard for people to live there or make long journeys across the region. Most of the Sahara is sand, but it does have *oasis* areas. An oasis is a fertile area in a desert where there is water and vegetation.

Sahara Desert

In parts of the Sahara Desert, it is normal for temperatures to reach well over 100°F during the daytime. The nighttimes can be extremely cold. The Sahara divides the continent into two regions: North Africa and sub-Saharan Africa.

THE KALAHARI DESERT

Another major desert in Africa is the **Kalahari Desert**. It covers about 100,000 square miles. The Kalahari stretches across much of southwestern Africa. The Kalahari is very dry and has extremely hot temperatures during the summer months. Thanks to underground water supplies, grass, shrubs, and a number of wild animals manage to live in the Kalahari Desert.

THE SAHEL

The **Sahel** is a belt of dry grasslands along the southern edge of the Sahara Desert. It runs through twelve countries. The Sahel's climate is semiarid. It gets more rainfall than the desert but still receives very little. At one time, enough rain fell in the Sahel to raise crops. In the 1970s, however, droughts (lack of rain) caused famine (lack of food). Many people starved. Farmers lost their livestock. Crops failed. Farmers had no seed to plant again when the rains returned. Many moved to the cities. The desert gradually took over the farmland the people left behind.

SAVANNAS

Lioness

Closer to the equator, the climate becomes hot. These areas have both rainy and dry seasons. **Savannas** cover the regions just north and south of the rainforests that lie along the equator. Savannas are hot, dry grasslands. In a savanna, the grass is tall and thick. Trees are short and scattered. Many of the wild animals associated with Africa, such as elephants, antelope, lions, and zebras, live in the savannas. Although the soil is rich, farming in the savannas is limited because of disease-carrying insects like the tsetse fly and the black fly.

Savanna

TROPICAL RAINFORESTS

Along the equator lies the Congo Basin, home to the world's second-largest tropical rainforest (only the Amazon in South America is bigger). A **tropical rainforest** is a forest close to the equator that averages over seventy inches of rain a year. Rainforests have dense vegetation. In the Congo, trees are so thick and tall that sunlight never reaches the forest floor. Thousands of different plants and animals live in the rainforest.

Tropical Rainforest

MAJOR RIVERS AND BODIES OF WATER

For centuries, bodies of water have played a crucial role in Africa. The oceans, seas, and rivers that surround and run through Africa have long served to unite Africans and provide access to the outside world. Long before the invention of trains, automobiles, or airplanes, rivers and oceans allowed Africans to engage in trade and gain exposure to new ideas. Major bodies of water that surround the continent are the Mediterranean Sea (north), the Red Sea (northeast), the Atlantic Ocean (west), and the Indian Ocean (east).

MAJOR RIVERS IN AFRICA

Several major rivers run through the interior of Africa. The **Nile River** is more than four thousand miles long and is the longest river in the world. For thousands of years, the Nile has provided a means of travel and a key source of water for parts of Africa. Much of Africa's most fertile farmland lies along the Nile River. Farmers have long relied on the river as a source of water to irrigate crops. Without the Nile, many nations would not be able to feed their populations.

Nile River

At almost three thousand miles long, the **Congo River** is the second longest in Africa. People use the Congo River for fishing and travel. Today, thanks to the Inga Dam, the Congo River produces large amounts of electricity for central Africa.

Millions of West Africans rely on the **Niger River** for food, water, and drainage. The Niger River begins in Guinea and flows northward through Mali, Niger, and Nigeria. During the rainy season, the river floods, creating freshwater marshlands. These marshlands provide fertile land for rice and abundant amounts of fish. Meanwhile, the Niger Delta contains rich supplies of oil, providing Nigeria with much of its annual income.

The **Zambezi River** is southern Africa's longest river. It has many waterfalls, including world-famous **Victoria Falls**. More than a mile across, the roar of the falls can be heard by people from nearly twenty miles away.

Victoria Falls

AFRICAN LAKES

Lake Victoria is the largest lake in Africa. It is the second-largest freshwater lake in the world (only Lake Superior in North America is bigger). It is roughly 26,800 square miles and extends into three countries: Tanzania, Uganda, and Kenya. Lake Victoria is very important. It provides a living for many fishermen and attracts millions of tourists each year.

Lake Tanganyika is a large lake in central Africa. It is the second-deepest freshwater lake in the world. Four countries share Lake Tanganyika: Burundi, Democratic Republic of Congo, Tanzania, and Zambia. Believed by scientists to contain over two hundred unique species of fish, Lake Tanganyika regularly attracts snorkelers and scuba divers from all over the world. Like Lake Victoria, it attracts tourism that boosts the local economies.

Lake Tanganyika

THE ATLAS MOUNTAINS

The **Atlas Mountains** are a mountain range in northwest Africa. The Atlas Mountains run through Morocco, Algeria, and Tunisia. This mountain range separates the Mediterranean and Atlantic coastlines from the Sahara Desert. Summers in the Atlas Mountains are very hot. Winters bring heavy snows. Because the Atlas Mountains lie within a fault zone (a place where different plates of the earth's crust meet and push together), they are prone to earthquakes. In 1980, an earthquake occurred in Algeria that killed five thousand people.

NATIONS IN AFRICA

Nations of Africa

SOUTH AFRICA

South Africa sits at the southern tip of Africa. Its coastline stretches more than fifteen hundred miles along both the Atlantic and Indian oceans. South Africa has a mild climate. The summers are not too hot, and the winters are not too cold.

South Africa is the most economically developed nation in Africa. The country has a large middle class and valuable natural resources. Gold and diamonds are abundant in South Africa. Interestingly, South Africa is also the only nation in the world with three capital cities. Cape Town, the largest of the three, is the legislative capital. Pretoria serves as the administrative capital. Bloemfontein provides the judicial capital.

Johannesburg, South Africa

SUDAN

Sudan is the largest country in Africa. It is in North Africa and borders the Red Sea. Sudan is flat with several mountain ranges. North Sudan is mostly dry desert, and experiences sand storms so thick that they occasionally block out all sunlight.

Sudan has large amounts of mineral resources. Petroleum and gold are major resources that help the country's economy. In recent years, Sudan has had ties to terrorism. **Terrorists** are people who harm property and/or kill innocent people in the name of a political cause. Al Qaeda leader Osama bin Laden lived in Sudan from 1992 to 1996. He later returned to Afghanistan to plan the notorious 9/11 terrorist attacks.

EGYPT

Egypt, in North Africa, is one of the most populated countries in Africa. The northern coast of Egypt borders the Mediterranean Sea. Many Egyptians live near the Nile River because of the fresh water and fertile farmland it provides. About half the population lives in urban areas like Cairo and Alexandria. Much of Egypt is desert with sand dunes (hills of sand) that occasionally reach heights of more than a hundred feet.

Pyramids

Archaeologists and historians flock to Egypt to study the remains of its ancient civilizations. Pyramids in which many of Egypt's most glorious pharaohs (ancient rulers of Egypt) lay buried are among the world's most famous attractions.

Tourism, international business, and trade are very important to Egypt's economy. The country also serves as an important political center, traditionally playing a major role among Arab nations in the Middle East.

Cairo

KENYA

Kenya is in eastern Africa. Near Kenya's coast lie fertile plains. The country has some of the most fertile land in Africa. Farmland, tropical rainforests, and swamps are in this region. Kenya also has dry plateaus (high flatlands), hills, and mountains.

Known for its wildlife, Kenya is home to lions, leopards, water buffalo, rhinoceros, and elephants. Its climate tends to be hot and humid along the coast, mild inland, and dry in the northern regions. Temperatures remain mild throughout the year, with rainy seasons occurring from April to June.

DEMOCRATIC REPUBLIC OF CONGO

The **Democratic Republic of Congo** is one-quarter the size of the United States and is the largest country in central Africa. French is the official language, but native languages are often spoken as well. Almost half of Africa's rainforests are found in the Democratic Republic of Congo.

People of Kenya

The country relies heavily on the Congo River for water and transportation. It is an unstable nation. Local fighting has killed more than four million people in Congo since 1998. The nation's economy depends on its diamond industry, rubber, and cobalt.

NIGERIA

Nigeria is located in western Africa. It borders several nations and the Atlantic Ocean. The country has a long history. People have lived in Nigeria since 9000 BC.

Nigeria has a large population. It is the most populous country in Africa. Nigeria is one of the poorest countries on earth. However, wealthier nations have invested more in Nigeria in recent years. The country also has a rich oil supply. As a result, Nigeria's economy is growing faster than ever before.

Life in Nigeria

Practice 1.1: Physical Features and Nations of Africa

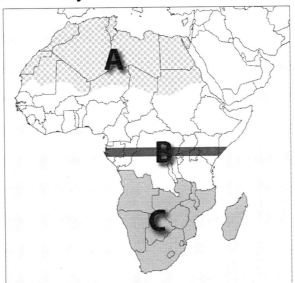

1. Which of the following would you find in area A on the map above?

   A. Sahara Desert

   B. tropical rainforests

   C. Kalahari Desert

   D. South Africa

2. Which of the following would you find in the area labeled B on the map above?

   A. tropical rainforests

   B. Egypt

   C. Atlas Mountains

   D. Sahel

3. Which country is the **largest** in Africa? Which one is the **most** populous?

1.2 ENVIRONMENTAL ISSUES FACING AFRICA

POLLUTION

Like other parts of the world, Africa must deal with environmental problems. One major problem facing Africa is **pollution.** Pollution occurs when human-made products or waste negatively alter the natural environment. Trash left in an open field, harmful chemicals released into the air by a factory, and industrial waste flowing into a natural water supply are all forms of pollution.

Pollution in Africa

WATER POLLUTION

Water pollution is a huge problem in Africa. Many parts of the continent have a limited water supply. Therefore, countries must be careful to protect what water they have. People depend on these water supplies for survival.

Farming methods often involve the use of fertilizers and pesticides. The chemicals in these products can pollute the water and make it unsafe to drink. Human waste also finds its way into water supplies. Mining is another problem. Explosions that unearth valuable minerals send dust and harmful debris into nearby water supplies. Human-made dams and industrial waste from urban areas also often pollute the water. Such contamination causes serious health problems in certain parts of Africa.

URBAN POLLUTION

Africa is home to many large cities. These urban areas have large populations, rail stations, factories, and tremendous amounts of traffic. While these cities help provide jobs and greater opportunity than more rural areas, they also produce a great deal of pollution.

Urban Africa

THE IMPACT OF EXTRACTION

Resources are things that people use. For example, money is a resource people use to buy things. **Natural resources** are resources produced by nature. Trees, water, oil, air, gold, coal, and many other things are natural resources. **Extraction** is the process of removing natural resources for use.

EXTRACTION'S IMPACT IN KENYA

Extraction impacts Africa. In Kenya, for example, wildlife is an abundant natural resource. For years, big-game hunting has lured millions to the country. Simultaneously, the meat from animals like the impala and water buffalo has been a source of economic income. Ivory from the tusks of elephants is also valuable. But mass hunting of these animals has disturbed the natural balance of wildlife. It has also left many animals as endangered species (in danger of no longer existing). To protect endangered species, the Kenyan government attempts to regulate the hunting of certain animals.

In addition, as the population grows and Kenya allows foreign countries to drill along its coast in search of oil, the country's wildlife could be increasingly affected.

Kenyan Hunter

EXTRACTION'S IMPACT IN CHAD

A poor and very dry country, Chad has few natural resources. However, it has rich oil supplies. A few years ago, Chad built a pipeline to better access its abundant oil.

While the pipeline has had economic benefit, many argue that it negatively impacted the environment. Parts of Chad's fertile, southern region were disturbed. Native peoples were displaced from lands they had occupied for generations. Today, many are concerned that the pipeline runs too close to Lake Chad. The lake is a major source of water in an already dry region. One spill from the pipeline could contaminate the lake and leave millions without the water they need to survive.

Chad Pipeline

EXTRACTION'S IMPACT ON NIGERIA

The impact of extraction on the environment is also evident in Nigeria. The Niger Delta is one of the world's largest wetlands. It is also home to Nigeria's major oil reserves. A poor country, Nigeria greatly depends on its oil. Unfortunately, oil drilling can damage the environment. In the Niger Delta, drilling has destroyed trees, killed plants, and displaced animals. Balancing the needs of people who need natural resources with the importance of maintaining a clean environment is one of Africa's greatest challenges.

Oil Drilling in Nigeria

WATER, DEFORESTATION, AND DESERTIFICATION

AFRICAN WATER SUPPLIES

Because much of Africa is dry, **water** is an important resource. Rivers like the Nile serve as crucial supplies of water for farming and daily survival. In Egypt, the Nile provides water for cities like Cairo and Alexandria. In Sudan, the Nile allows farmers and herdsmen to get the water they need to provide food for the population. Mali depends on the Niger River. Without any large rivers, the desert nation of Chad relies on Lake Chad for survival.

African Farming

Water is not evenly distributed throughout Africa. Parts of Africa are very dry. People in these regions depend on the few rivers or lakes that exist in these regions. Many live as nomads. They move from place to place in search of fresh water supplies. The few farmers who live in dry regions must raise crops that need little water or rely on irrigation. **Irrigation** is a human-made process by which water is carried from water supplies to dry areas.

Other parts of Africa are very wet. They lie along large rivers or within rainforests. Flooding and heavy rains can be concerns in these areas. The amount of water in a region often determines the way different people live and how they make their livings.

DEFORESTATION

Deforestation is the process of destroying rainforests to make way for human development. As more vegetation is destroyed, animals retreat further into the shrinking forests. Some species even become extinct (no longer exist). In addition, native peoples who have depended on the rainforests for centuries find their way of life disrupted forever.

Deforestation has environmental effects as well. As the number of trees shrinks, so does the amount of oxygen they produce. Meanwhile, the amount of carbon dioxide in the air increases. Fewer rainforests also mean fewer medicines. About one-fourth of all medicines people use come from rainforest plants.

People destroy forests to make room for homes, industries, roads, farmland, and so on. The results have sometimes been devastating. Without enough trees, rainfall cannot be trapped. The water moves to the surface faster and causes floods. Deforestation also causes droughts. Many plants and animals die. Many African countries now have policies in place to protect their forests and wildlife. Kenya has turned much of its land into wildlife parks, where hunting is illegal. Other nations, like South Africa and Mali, have passed laws placing strict limitations on the amount of forest land that can be cleared each year.

DESERTIFICATION

In areas where deserts exist, desertification is a problem. **Desertification** is the process of previously fertile land becoming desert. Limited rain, poor farming techniques that strip the soil of nutrients, and extended droughts are some of the causes of desertification. Desertification severely lessens the amount of food available and contributes to famines.

Desertification

Practice 1.2: Environmental Issues Facing Africa

1. Removing natural resources so that people can use them is called

    A. deforestation.

    B. infiltration.

    C. extraction.

    D. desertification.

2. What are some of the environmental challenges facing Africa?

1.3 HOW GEOGRAPHY IMPACTS PEOPLE

THE IMPACT OF PHYSICAL FEATURES

Physical features impact economy, population, development, and culture. Mountainous regions and deserts have harsher terrains. They are less populated than fertile areas. Regions with lots of water attract larger numbers of people. They have more commerce, industrialization, and urbanization than secluded, dry areas. Rivers and deltas provide rich farmland and produce more agricultural products than semiarid areas. Rainforests tend to be less populated and their inhabitants more primitive because of thick vegetation that limits travel and contact with the outside world.

THE SAHARA AND SAHEL

Because it is a vast desert, the Sahara makes life challenging. The majority of those who live in this area raise sheep, goats, and camels. People who live in the Sahara tend to be nomadic (move from location to location) because they must constantly find water and grazing areas. They often live in tents that can be easily carried from place to place. They often travel by camel in caravans (a group that travels together). Camels are big enough to carry much of what desert inhabitants need and require very little water for survival. Caravans provide protection from bandits who might otherwise attack desert travelers. Many people who live in the Sahel are also nomadic herders.

Bedouin Nomads

SAVANNAS

Many African people live in the savannas. Because trees
are scarce, their homes are often made out of grass and
twigs. They are often cattle herders. Because water is more
abundant, savanna peoples are typically less nomadic than
people in the Sahara and Sahel. If they migrate (move
from one place to another), they tend to do so according to
predictable wet and dry seasons.

Savanna People

TROPICAL RAINFORESTS

Some people live in the tropical rainforests. One such group is
the Pygmies. Averaging around four feet tall, Pygmies are
some of the shortest people on earth. As hunters and gatherers,
their small size allows them to move about comfortably in the
thick rainforests.

ETHNIC AND RELIGIOUS GROUPS OF AFRICA

There are many different ethnic groups and religious groups in
Africa. **Ethnic groups** are based on biology. Race, physical
features, ancestry, and so on determine a person's ethnic group.
Different ethnic groups in Africa include Arabs, Bantu
peoples, white Africans, Swahili, and many others.

Pygmies

Religious groups are based on religion. Christians, Muslims, Jews, followers of native African
religions, and various other religious groups live in Africa. People from different ethnic groups
are often members of the same religious group.

Some religions may be more popular among certain ethnic groups than others. However, just
because people are part of a certain ethnic group doesn't mean they automatically belong to a
certain religious group. Not all white people are Christian or Jewish. Not all black Africans hold
to native African faiths. Just because people are Arabs doesn't mean that they are Muslim.
People can be part of the same ethnic group, but have different religious beliefs. At the same
time, people can be part of the same religious group, but have different ethnic backgrounds.

ARABS

North African nations like Egypt and Morocco
have large **Arab** populations. Arab peoples have
dark brown complexions. Islam tends to be the
main religion among Arab peoples, although other
religions are practiced. The Arab cultures of North
Africa are similar to those of Southwest Asian
peoples like the Iraqis.

North African (Afro-Arabs)

Over the centuries, many Arabs have married and had children with black Africans. Their descendants form an ethnic group known as **Afro-Arabs**. Their culture is a mixture of Arab and various black African traditions.

BANTU PEOPLES

Bantu peoples include a variety of ethnic groups that share similar languages and are believed to descend from common ancestors. Originally, most Bantu peoples came from Central Africa. However, over thousands of years, Bantu peoples migrated south and, today, make up a large portion of southern Africa's population.

The Bantu people impacted Africa in many ways. They brought with them advanced forms of agriculture and iron tools that transformed much of southern Africa from a hunting-gathering society into a farming and herding society. One of the largest population movements in human history, the Bantu migration is believed to have begun around 1000 BC and lasted into the fourth century AD.

For years, South Africa's white government tried to justify many of its racist policies by insisting that white settlers and black Bantus arrived in southern Africa at about the same time. They argued that this gave both groups equal claim to the land. Evidence now shows, however, that Bantus and other native Africans were living in southern Africa long before the first whites arrived.

Bantu Migration

ASHANTI

The **Ashanti** people formed a powerful West African empire before European colonization. Today, they are a major ethnic group in the country of Ghana. Ashanti peoples practice a number of traditional African religions. However, Christianity is the predominant religion among most Ashanti today.

Ashanti People

SWAHILI

The **Swahili** people live along the coast of East Africa. Kenya, Tanzania, and Mozambique all have sizeable Swahili populations. The Swahili culture has greatly impacted Africa. Many Africans who are not Swahili speak some form of the Swahili language.

Sometime during the eleventh century, Islam spread to East Africa. Today, most Swahili people are Muslim. However, many traditional faiths and other religions are practiced among the Swahili too.

Swahili People

LITERACY

Literacy is the ability to read and write. Due to generations of colonization and oppression, much of Africa's population is illiterate. (Chapter 3 discusses the European colonization of Africa.) Illiteracy makes it hard for people to get good jobs. Low literacy makes it difficult for African nations to compete economically with more educated European, Asian, and American countries. This keeps many African nations poor and the standard of living low.

Traditional Yorubas

In recent decades, African governments have applied greater effort to increasing Africa's literacy rate. In many nations, more Africans attend school than in the past. Africa owes its independence to literacy and education. Many of the nationalist independence movements discussed in chapter 2 were led by educated Africans.

African School

Practice 1.3: How Geography Impacts People

1. Where would one expect to find the **largest** population of people?

    A. an African urban area

    B. the Sahara Desert

    C. a tropical rainforest

    D. the savanna

2. Define the difference between an ethnic group and a religious group.

3. How does illiteracy affect people in Africa?

CHAPTER 1 REVIEW

Key Terms

geography
deserts
Sahara Desert
Kalahari Desert
Sahel
savannas
tropical rainforest
Nile River
Congo River
Niger River
Zambezi River
Victoria Falls
Lake Victoria
Lake Tanganyika
Atlas Mountains
South Africa
Sudan
terrorists
Egypt
Kenya

Democratic Republic of Congo
Nigeria
pollution
resources
natural resources
extraction
water
irrigation
deforestation
desertification
impact of physical features
ethnic groups
religious groups
Arabs
Afro-Arabs
Bantu
Ashanti
Swahili
literacy

Chapter Review Questions

1. A large, dry area that stretches across North Africa and is very difficult to live in or cross is the
   A. Kalahari Desert.
   B. rainforest.
   C. Sahara Desert.
   D. Nile River.

2. Which of the following people migrated from central to southern Africa over thousands of years, bringing with them advanced tools, herding techniques, and agriculture?
   A. Europeans
   B. Pygmies
   C. Arabs
   D. Bantus

3. Oil drilling, industrialization, traffic, and growing cities can cause
   A. desertification.
   B. famines.
   C. religion.
   D. pollution.

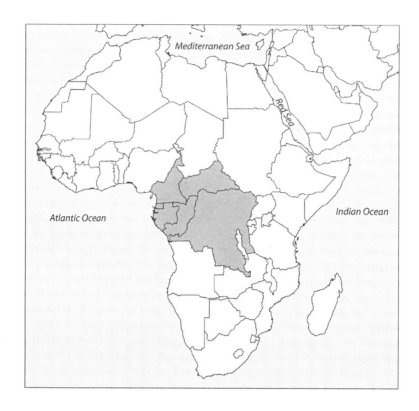

4. Who of the following people would you **most likely** find living in the area shaded on the map above?

   A. Pygmies

   B. Arabs

   C. Nomads

   D. white South Africans

5. When rainforests shrink because of human development, it is called

   A. desertification.

   B. deforestation.

   C. reforestation.

   D. rainforest duplication.

6. What African region is depicted in the photograph above?
   A. rainforest

   B. Nile River

   C. savanna

   D. Sahara Desert

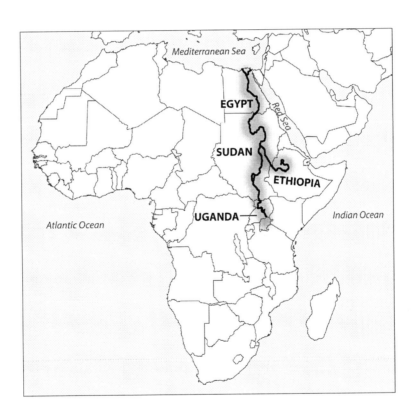

7. Which river is depicted on the map above?
   A. Nile River

   B. Congo River

   C. Niger River

   D. Zambezi River

8. Which of the following would **likely** impact a farmer in Egypt the most?

   A. mining in South Africa

   B. desertification in western Africa

   C. a dam on the Nile River

   D. tourism at Lake Victoria

9. Hakeem and Abja are both Muslims. Hakeem is black and lives in Somalia. Abja is Arab and lives in Egypt. Hakeem and Abja are members of the same

   A. ethnic group.

   B. religious group.

   C. nationality.

   D. family group.

10. Read question #9 again. Hakeem and Abja are members of different

   A. ethnic groups.

   B. religious groups.

   C. continents.

   D. faiths.

Chapter 2
Historical Understandings of Africa

This chapter covers the following Georgia standard.

SS7H1	The student will analyze continuity and change in Africa leading to the 21st century.

2.1 EARLY AFRICA AND EUROPEAN COLONIZATION

EARLY AFRICAN CULTURE

CULTURE

Africa is the world's second-largest continent and is home to many different peoples and cultures. Most historians and archaeologists believe that the first humans lived in Africa. The earliest Africans were hunters and gatherers who traveled from place to place in search of food. Later, Africans began to settle and build farming and herding communities. Major rivers, like the Nile, Niger, and Congo, allowed people to travel and carry on trade with outside groups.

Early African

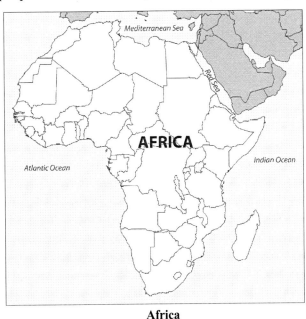

Africa

TRADE AND SLAVES

Trade routes also stretched over land. At first, mules and oxen carried many traded goods. However, around the first century AD, traders began to use camels that were better adapted to travel across the continent's vast deserts. People in other regions eagerly sought the gold, copper, salt, and ivory that African traders provided. Africans also made money trading slaves (people who are owned like property, have no rights, and are bought and sold the way you would buy or sell a car). In

Early African Slaves

Africa, some cultures would force prisoners of war to serve their captors as slaves or would sell them as slaves to foreign peoples.

Trade opened Africa to the rest of the world. Across the Indian Ocean to the east, African civilizations traded and interacted with Asian societies. To the north, across the Mediterranean Sea, awaited Europe and parts of Southwest Asia. Beyond the Red Sea sat the Arabian Peninsula. Eventually, trade (especially in African slaves) stretched across the Atlantic Ocean as well.

Before Europeans arrived and began to conquer parts of Africa, a number of African societies grew wealthy and powerful. Much of their prosperity was due to agricultural development and trade with other civilizations.

AFRICAN EMPIRES

Several great empires developed in Africa before Europeans arrived. Ghana, Mali, and Songhai arose in western Africa. Nubia and Ethiopia arose in eastern Africa. These empires featured powerful leaders, thriving trade, impressive cities, and centers of knowledge and commerce.

EUROPEAN COLONIZATION

Beginning in the nineteenth century, Europeans aggressively established colonies in Africa. A **colony** is an area claimed by a country in a foreign territory. Europeans wanted to control African territories and the wealth their resources produced. European powers used their superior military strength to conquer and colonize parts of Africa. Great Britain, France, Germany, Belgium, the Netherlands, and Portugal all established colonies in Africa.

Pre-European African Empire

THE BERLIN CONFERENCE

In 1884, German chancellor Otto von Bismarck hosted the **Berlin Conference**. In Berlin, the major European powers laid down guidelines regarding European claims to African territories. They officially recognized German and British claims in eastern Africa and awarded Mozambique to Portugal. Without including any Africans in their discussions, the representatives to the Berlin Conference divided up Africa among themselves, as if the native Africans who lived there had no claim to the land at all.

German Chancellor Otto Von Bismarck

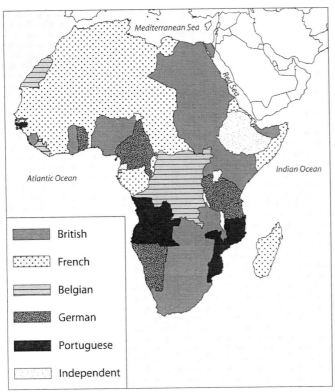

Colonies After Berlin Conference

ARTIFICIAL BOUNDARIES

The Berlin Conference drew **artificial boundaries**. It did not divide Africa based on where different ethnic groups had lived for generations. Rather, it divided the continent based on available resources the different European nations wanted. As a result, many people groups were divided. Often, they were forced to co-exist with other groups they had long considered enemies. Combined with the resentment many Africans felt toward European colonizers, these conflicts often led to unrest and violence. Even today, these artificial boundaries continue to contribute to instability and civil wars.

Practice 2.1: Early African and European Colonization

1. What was the purpose of the Berlin Conference?

2. How did artificial boundaries affect colonial Africa?

2.2 NATIONALIST MOVEMENTS AND INDEPENDENCE

AFRICAN NATIONALISM

For decades, most of Africa remained under European rule. During World War I, many Africans fought in the armies of European nations in the hope of being rewarded with independence. These people were disappointed to find that Africa still rested under the thumb of European leaders after the war.

In protest, many Africans organized **nationalist movements**. These movements called for independent African states. Blacks in South Africa and Nigeria formed trade unions. In Kenya, protest resulted in violent retaliation by the government and the exile of the independence movement's leader. France crushed a revolt in Morocco. Italy unleashed all its military fierceness to end an uprising in Libya. Despite such violence and bloodshed, African independence movements grew in the years leading up to World War II.

Eventually, European nations realized they could not hold on to their colonies. By the end of the 1960s, nearly every European nation had granted independence to nations in Africa. Only Portugal resisted. By 1974, even the Portuguese had no choice but to give up control.

**Nationalist Leader
of Ghana
Kwame Nkrumah**

THE PAN-AFRICAN MOVEMENT

Increased education helped fuel these nationalist movements. A nationalist movement is one inspired by pride in one's country and people. Many of the leaders calling for African independence were black Africans who had been educated overseas in Europe or the United States.

**National Leader of
Congo
Patrice Lumumba**

Calls for African independence spread across the continent following World War II. It created a unified movement known as Pan-Africanism. The **Pan-African movement** called for all black Africans to see themselves as a united people in their fight against European colonization.

The Pan-African movement led to the founding of the **African Union** in 2001. The African Union seeks to unite Africans in an effort to improve conditions across the continent. Economic growth, the end of poverty and starvation, advancement of women's rights, improved education, and the end of African wars are among its noblest goals.

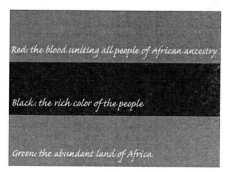

Red: the blood uniting all people of African ancestry

Black: the rich color of the people

Green: the abundant land of Africa

Pan-African Flag

KENYAN INDEPENDENCE MOVEMENT

In Kenya, independence did not come peacefully. By 1952, the country was rocked with violence between black laborers and white landowners. Great Britain used its military power to put down the African protests. Eventually, imprisoned nationalist leader, Jomo Kenyatta, re-emerged to lead the **Kenyan independence movement** in the early 1960s. In 1963, Kenya won its independence. The following year, Kenyatta became president.

NIGERIAN INDEPENDENCE MOVEMENT

In 1960, several African nations, including British Nigeria and Belgian Congo, achieved independence. The **Nigerian independence movement** owed much of its success to a Nigerian youth movement that began in the 1930s and trained many of its future leaders. These leaders

Jomo Kenyatta of Kenya

effectively put pressure on Great Britain to grant their nation independence. Not wanting a repeat of the bloodshed in Kenya, Great Britain bowed to pressure from nationalist leaders and agreed to peacefully surrender its claims to Nigeria.

SOUTH AFRICA'S HISTORY, INDEPENDENCE, AND ANTI-APARTHEID MOVEMENTS

PRE-INDEPENDENCE

South Africa's colonial history impacted the nation well into the twentieth century. By the mid-1600s, the Netherlands was the dominant European sea power. It exercised control over many of the trade routes between Europe and Southeast Asia. The Dutch established a small colony at the Cape of Good Hope (southernmost tip of Africa). It was meant to serve as a port where trading ships on their way to Asia could stop for supplies.

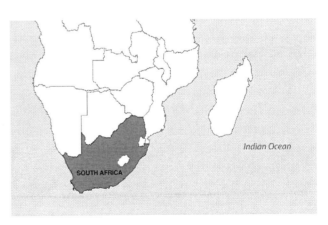

South Africa

Eventually, the Cape grew into a much larger colony: **South Africa**. As European colonists received parcels of land from the Dutch government, they began to take over territories once occupied by native Africans. They forced local Africans to work for them or imported slaves from Asia or other parts of the continent.

In 1795, the Dutch monarch invited Great Britain to take over control of South Africa. This caused great tension between white British colonists and Afrikaners (white colonists of Dutch descent). Both nationalities, however, oppressed black Africans. Later, as people became aware of the gold and diamonds in the region, violent conflicts arose.

Colonial South Africa

From 1899 to 1902, Great Britain and Afrikaners fought one another in the South African War (also known as the Boer War). In 1902, British forces defeated the Afrikaners and established control over South Africa's gold and diamond producing regions. They allowed many Afrikaners to keep their land, however, and maintained policies denying blacks equality. In 1910, the territory officially became the Union of South Africa. As a dominion, it remained part of the British Empire but was allowed to govern itself. Over time, its minority white population tightened its grip more and more, severely limiting the rights of blacks.

INDEPENDENCE AND APARTHEID

> **CITY OF DURBAN**
>
> UNDER SECTION 37 OF THE DURBAN BEACH BY-LAWS, THIS BATHING AREA IS RESERVED FOR THE SOLE USE OF MEMBERS OF THE WHITE RACE GROUP.

Apartheid Sign

South Africa followed a unique path to independence. Following the South African War, racial segregation increased. In 1948, Afrikaners won control of South Africa's government. They then established an official policy of racial discrimination called **apartheid**. Apartheid stripped black South Africans of the few rights they had and required segregation (separation) based on race. It resulted in most blacks living in poverty and providing cheap labor for whites.

Many blacks attempted to resist racism. In 1912, a group of black South Africans founded the **African National Congress (ANC)**. The ANC tried to unify blacks to resist white policies. After apartheid, however, the ANC's task became more difficult. In 1961, South Africa became an independent republic (of course, only whites could vote). Three years later, the government sentenced the ANC's most famous leader, **Nelson Mandela**, to life in prison. Apartheid remained the official policy of South Africa for more than thirty years.

APARTHEID ENDS

Mandela as a Young Man

During the 1970s, pressures began to force the end of apartheid. White business owners needed black workers. They called for an end to restrictions that prevented them from hiring more blacks. Meanwhile, other countries began to impose trade sanctions against South Africa.

Nelson Mandela as President

Finally, in 1990, a progressive South African president named **F.W. de Klerk** began dismantling apartheid, and had Nelson Mandela released. Four years later, the ANC won control of the national government in a democratic election and Mandela became president of South Africa. He served until 1999.

F.W. de Klerk

Although more economically developed than many African nations, South Africa continues to face challenges. Much of its majority black population remains poor and far less educated than white South Africans. Unemployment and AIDS remain major concerns. Still, the end of apartheid at least allows black South Africans more opportunities than they have enjoyed since Europeans arrived centuries ago.

Practice 2.2: Nationalist Movements and Independence

1. What did African nationalist movements strive for?

2. What did the Pan-African movement call for?

3. Describe the roles played by Nelson Mandela and F.W. de Klerk in ending apartheid in South Africa.

CHAPTER 2 REVIEW

Key Terms

colony
Berlin Conference
artificial boundaries
nationalist movements
Pan-African movement
African Union
Nigerian independence movement

Kenyan independence movement
South Africa
Afrikaners
apartheid
ANC
Nelson Mandela
F.W. de Klerk

Chapter Review Questions

1. Prior to African independence, many European nations established

   A. nationalist movements.

   B. a Pan-African conference.

   C. colonies.

   D. the Berlin movement.

2. How did the Berlin Conference impact Africa?

   A. The conference established apartheid.

   B. The conference established artificial boundaries that divided ethnic groups and still lead to conflict in Africa today.

   C. The conference removed all European powers from Africa except Portugal, who did not give up control until the 1970s.

   D. The conference began the Pan-African movement because it was led by black Africans who wanted to fight for independence.

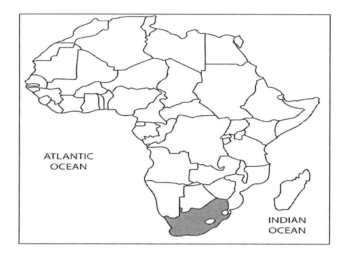

3. Who of the following is associated with the shaded area in the map above?

   A. Otto von Bismarck   C. Jomo Kenyatta

   B. Nelson Mandela   D. none of the above

4. Which of the following called for black Africans to unite in their struggle against European colonizers?

   A. the Berlin Conference   C. Pan-African movement

   B. apartheid   D. colonial movement

5. How did apartheid affect blacks in South Africa?

   A. Apartheid gave blacks equal rights in South Africa.

   B. Apartheid gave Great Britain control of South Africa.

   C. Apartheid did not affect South Africa because it was a policy in Kenya.

   D. Apartheid oppressed blacks and left many of them in poverty.

6. What role did youth movements play in Nigeria's independence movement?

   A. major role   C. no role

   B. minor role   D. none of the above

Chapter 3
Political and Economic Understandings of Africa

This chapter covers the following Georgia standards.

SS7CG1	The student will compare and contrast various forms of government.
SS7CG2	The student will explain the structures of the modern governments of Africa.
SS7CG3	The student will analyze how politics in Africa impacts standard of living.
SS7E1	The student will analyze different economic systems.
SS7E2	The student will explain how voluntary trade benefits buyers and sellers in Africa.
SS7E3	The student will describe factors that influence economic growth and examine their presence or absence in Nigeria and South Africa.

3.1 FORMS OF GOVERNMENT

CONFEDERATIONS, FEDERATIONS, AND UNITARY GOVERNMENTS

UNITARY GOVERNMENTS

There are different forms of government. Some countries have a **unitary government**. A single national government has all the power. There is no state or local government independent of the national government.

CONFEDERATIONS

Some governments are a **confederation**. They are made up of various provincial or state governments. There is a loose national alliance between them. However, most of the power is with the provincial or state governments. The national government has some power, but the smaller governments within the confederation have a great deal of freedom.

Hosni Mubarak
President of Egypt

FEDERATIONS

A **federation** is a government in which a strong national government shares power with provincial or state governments. Most of the power is in the hands of the national government, but some authority is reserved for the state or province. The United States is a federation. The federal (national) government shares power with fifty state governments.

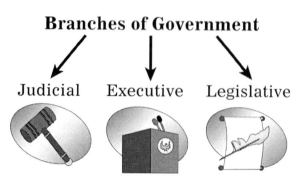

AUTOCRATIC, OLIGARCHIC, AND DEMOCRATIC GOVERNMENTS

AUTOCRACIES

Some governments are **autocracies**. They are ruled by one self-appointed ruler or dictator. Citizens do not have much say in an autocracy. The ruler usually does what he or she wants. He or she does not need the approval of the people. Autocratic leaders rule until they die, are overthrown, or decide to resign from office. Many rule for years or even decades.

Muammar al Gaddafi
Autocratic Leader of Libya

OLIGARCHIES

Oligarchies are governments that are ruled by a small group. Elite families, military officers, religious leaders, and/or members of the upper class often lead oligarchies. Those who are a part of the dominant group have a say in how the government is run. But citizens who are part of the lower class or who are outside the ruling group have very little say.

DEMOCRACIES

In **democracies**, citizens have a voice in their government. They elect their leaders and often get to vote on laws. If the people do not like their leaders, they can vote to replace them through elections. The United States is a democracy. People of all classes who are qualified citizens are allowed to vote and have a say in their government.

Citizen Voting in Democracy

FORMS OF DEMOCRATIC GOVERNMENT

PARLIAMENTARY DEMOCRACY

There are two major forms of democratic government: parliamentary systems and presidential systems. In a **parliamentary system**, power rests predominantly with a legislative body or parliament. The parliament selects government ministers. It also elects a **prime minister** who serves as both the leader of the legislature and the nation's head of government.

South African Parliament

The people have a say in their government through parliamentary elections. They elect members of parliament who will then choose government leaders. Often, there is also a head of state, such as a president or a monarch (king or queen). But the head of state has very little power.

PRESIDENTIAL DEMOCRACY

In a **presidential system**, power is divided between the legislature and an executive, usually called the **president**. The people elect their legislators and the president separately. The president and the legislature have clearly defined powers. They work together, but neither has authority over the other. The United States is a presidential democracy.

Mwai Kibaki
President of Kenya

Practice 3.1: Forms of Government

1. Who of the following would be the head of government in an autocracy?

   A. president

   B. dictator

   C. prime minister

   D. members of the upper class

2. Maria lives in a country where one national government has all the power. It sounds like Maria lives under which form of government?

   A. unitary

   B. federation

   C. confederation

   D. parliamentary autocracy

3. Which of the following is the **best** description of a prime minister?

   A. an executive independent of the legislative branch

   B. an autocratic ruler

   C. the leader of an elite ruling class

   D. a head of government elected by members of a legislature

3.2 GOVERNMENT AND POLITICS IN AFRICA

KENYA

Kenya's government is a presidential democracy. Its government is led by an elected president. The president acts as both head of state and head of government. The people elect the president to a five-year term. The elected president chooses the vice president and cabinet members from Kenya's legislative body, the National Assembly. The National Assembly is unicameral (has only one house).

SOUTH AFRICA

South Africa's government is a federation and a democratic government. It combines aspects of both a presidential and a parliamentary democracy. South Africa has three levels of government: national, provincial, and local. The national government is divided into three branches: legislative, executive, and judicial. The executive branch consists of the president, deputy president, speaker of the National Assembly, and the governmental ministers.

The president is the leader of the party with the most seats in the National Assembly and acts as the head of government. The president is also the head of state. The legislative branch is composed of a bicameral (two-house) parliament. The first house is called the National Assembly and consists of elected officials. The second house, known as the National Council of Provinces, consists of ninety officials appointed by provincial legislatures.

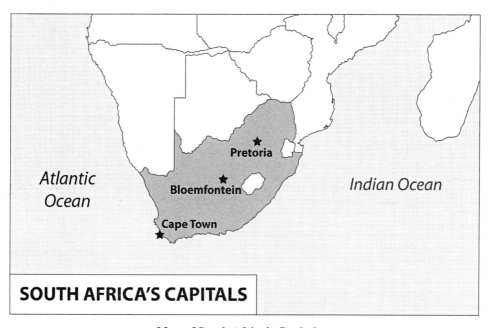

Map of South Africa's Capitals

SUDAN

Sudan's government is an autocratic system. It is led by President Omar al-Bashir. President al-Bashir has led the government since overthrowing Sudan's former leader in 1989. Officials restructured the government in 2005 as part of a peace agreement meant to end a civil war. The agreement was supposed to make the government more democratic. In reality, al-Bashir kept most of his power.

People in Sudan have very little say in their government. Sudan's president has often had people who oppose him imprisoned or even executed.

ACCESS TO EDUCATION

EDUCATION IN SUDAN

Education in Sudan is limited. Most schools are located in urban areas. Many schools in rural areas have been destroyed by fighting and civil war. In some areas, slightly less than half of the school-age children actually get a formal education. In certain areas, it is less than twenty percent.

School-Age Girl in Sudan

Traditionally, girls in Sudan have received less education than boys. Many Sudanese parents fear that education will corrupt their daughters. Girls are expected to be wives and mothers and to take care of the home or to help farm. Many in Sudan do not see a need for girls to receive a formal education. Although the educational opportunities for women are greater today than in the past, they are still very limited.

The predominant religion in Sudan is Islam. In 1990, Sudan reformed its educational system. Much of its curriculum is now based on Islamic law.

EDUCATION IN KENYA

Education in Kenya is influenced greatly by its colonial history. Kenya's educational system is based on the British model. Most young children attend primary schools. However, less than 30 percent attend secondary schools, and less than 5 percent go on to college or universities.

School in Kenya

The number of children attending school in Kenya has greatly increased since the government started offering free education in 2003. Unfortunately, free education has also led to overcrowded schools and a shortage of teachers. Kenya has private schools as well.

Despite the problems, Kenya's education system is improving. More and more students are getting an education. Many foreign nations, like Great Britain, have invested money to help support Kenya's educational system.

POLITICAL INSTABILITY

CIVIL WARS

Many African nations have experienced political instability, internal conflict, and civil wars since gaining their independence. **Civil wars** are wars that occur within one country. They are usually fought for control of the government.

Civil War

Four key factors lead to conflicts and civil wars in Africa. One is *poverty*. The more poverty exists in a country, the more citizens are dissatisfied. Widespread unhappiness leads to political instability.

Secondly, Africa's *population* continues to grow at a rapid rate. Population growth stretches Africa's scarce economic resources. Scarce resources create more discontent.

Third, Africa's dependence on precious n*atural resources* makes control of these resources a key to power and survival. Such conditions often erupt into violence and bloodshed.

Finally, Africa is home to many *different ethnic groups*. When European nations colonized parts of Africa, they drew borders based on agreements with other colonizing nations. They did not give much consideration to where different ethnic groups lived. As a result, these boundaries separated ethnic groups. Many had to live in countries with other ethnic groups they considered enemies. Today, these groups still mistrust one another. Often, they end up fighting wars for control of the countries in which they live.

Civil wars destroy land, homes, crops, and lives. Often, they involve ethnic fighting between tribes with long-standing rivalries. **Refugees** (people fleeing a country to escape war or some other catastrophic event) wind up homeless, starving, and contributing to the overpopulation of neighboring countries. Not only do civil wars contribute to political instability, they also keep Africa locked in poverty.

Refugees

Political instability also makes it difficult for nations to address other challenges. Many people in Africa face poverty, starvation, and health challenges. When civil wars and violence break out, it makes it harder to get food, medicines, and other needed supplies to those who are hurting. In addition, money and other resources that could go to ease suffering go to obtain weapons. Civil wars and instability create additional suffering. More people are made homeless. Schools are destroyed, increasing illiteracy and contributing to poverty. Crops are destroyed, creating more starvation. And people are killed, leaving children as orphans and families incomplete.

FAMINE, AIDS, AND ECONOMIC CHALLENGES

ECONOMIC CHALLENGES

At the time they achieved their freedom from European colonizers, most African societies relied mostly on agriculture and lagged far behind the western world economically. Many depended on one main product. For some, it was agricultural goods. For others, it was oil or some other natural resource. If crops were destroyed or prices for such goods dropped, entire nations suffered terribly. What resources many African nations did possess went to buy weapons for the military or to make corrupt leaders rich. As a result, African nations have had a difficult time developing economically.

Economic development occurs when nations become more industrialized, produce more goods, attract more financial investments, and create more wealth for the nation's population. Today, in many African nations, people have to resort to crime or bribery (paying for political favors) just to survive.

FAMINES

Famines (lack of food) are another major problem in Africa. Large portions of Africa have to deal with droughts (not enough rain) that cause crops to fail and lead to mass starvation. As Africa's population continues to grow faster than the continent can develop economically, many countries are simply unable to feed all their people. Ethiopia, Somalia, and Sudan are just a few of the areas in Africa commonly ravaged by famines.

Effects of Famine

AIDS

AIDS (Acquired Immune Deficiency Syndrome) is a disease that has devastated much of Africa. AIDS is spread through blood and other body fluids. It attacks the immune system, eventually leaving its victim unable to fight off infections and dying of disease. There is no known cure for AIDS.

Over the last three decades, AIDS has spread through Africa at an alarming rate. Millions of sub-Saharan Africans have been infected with the AIDS virus. (Sub-Saharan Africa is the part of Africa south of the Sahara Desert.) Roughly a third of all AIDS deaths worldwide occur in Africa. Many of those who die are children. The rate of infection is due largely to poverty and poor education. People are often unaware of how to prevent the spread of the disease and lack the resources to battle it once they become infected. The devastation caused by AIDS makes it even harder for African nations to grow economically and provide the kind of education and health care they need.

**AIDS Sufferers
in Africa**

Practice 3.2: Government and Politics in Africa

1. Describe Kenya's government. Describe South Africa's government. How are they similar? How are they different?

2. What kind of government does Sudan have?

3. What are four key factors that lead to conflict and civil wars in Africa? How do such conflicts and civil wars impact Africa's population?

4. How have famine and AIDS impacted Africa?

3.3 AFRICA'S ECONOMIC SYSTEMS

DIFFERENT ECONOMIC SYSTEMS

Economics is the study of how people, businesses, and countries use limited resources, such as money and materials. There are different types of economic systems. Each attempts to answer **three basic economic questions**:

What to produce?

How to produce?

For whom to produce?

TRADITIONAL ECONOMIES

Traditional economies are economies in which people usually produce just what they need to survive. If land is owned by anyone, it is usually by a wealthy ruling class.

People in a traditional economy inherit their position from their parents and are not expected to socially advance. Farmers remain farmers, herders remain herders, craftsmen remain craftsmen, and so on. People are motivated to produce in a traditional society by the need to survive and a sense of pride.

Traditional Economy

In many rural parts of Africa, tribal communities still depend to a certain degree on traditional economies. Countries, however, revolve around more-developed economic systems.

COMMAND ECONOMIES

In **command economies**, the government owns the means of production. Most businesses and property belong to the state rather than private businesses or individuals. The government decides what will be produced and in what amount.

Less-Developed Command Economy

The goal of command economies is economic equality. They are designed to keep people from becoming too rich or too poor. Unfortunately, command economies are often just as susceptible to greed and corruption as other economies.

Command economies have proved to be inefficient. The government determines what to produce, how to produce, and for whom to produce. The government often commands businesses to produce things that people do not want to buy. There is often not enough of the products people want (**shortage**) and too much of things people don't want (**surplus**).

Also, command economies often limit the amount of money people can make. Workers do not have the motivation of becoming wealthy or getting promoted if they work hard. As a result, workers in a command economy are often not as productive as in other economies.

In addition, the government often limits how much money businesses can make. There is no financial reward for producing better products. Therefore, command economies don't encourage the kind of economic development that comes with market economies.

Despite the pitfalls, many Africans have, at times, supported command economies. Many Africans live in extreme poverty. They are attracted to command economies because of their promise to bring economic relief to poor populations. Unfortunately, command economies fail to deliver the economic equality they are supposed to. Often, they increase poverty rather than relieve it.

MARKET ECONOMIES

Market economies allow for private ownership of businesses and property. Such economic systems are often called "capitalist" because they encourage **capitalism** (private ownership of property and the pursuit of profits in business). They have very little government regulation. Market demand determines what will be produced, rather than the government.

Market Economy

A **market** involves buyers and sellers exchanging money and goods. When you buy a new shirt or a DVD, you are exchanging money in an economic market. In market economies, businesses are free to produce what they choose, and buyers are free to buy what they want. The good thing about market economies is that they tend to operate more efficiently than command economies. Since businesses want to make money, they produce only what the market demands. Therefore, if people want shirts, then producers will make shirts until demand is satisfied. Shortages and surpluses usually don't last very long in market economies.

Capitalism

Market economies also produce innovation (new and better ways of doing things). Since businesses are competing with each other, they are always finding ways to make products better or invent new things. To do this, they try to hire the most qualified employees. Therefore, they tend to pay more money to workers who are skilled and do a good job. Workers have an incentive to work hard and obtain more training because it means more personal wealth for them. All this means that economic development tends to occur much faster in market economies than in command or traditional economies.

The downside of market economies is that they often produce "haves" and "have nots." Since financial success depends on one's ability to respond to market demands, market societies tend to consist of a few rich people, a large middle class, and a poor lower class. There is no guarantee of equality in a market economy.

MIXED ECONOMIES

In reality, most economies are **mixed economies**. They are not totally command or totally market. They have elements of both. Some mixed economies lean more towards free markets, and some lean more towards command structures. For instance, the United States is not totally a market society. The government places some regulations on businesses, monitors how stocks are traded, outlaws monopolies, and will intervene if inflation gets out of control. Overall, however, it tries to let the market operate as freely as possible.

China, on the other hand, places strict control on its economy, and many of the larger industries are owned by the state. In recent years, however, its desire to compete economically has led it to allow some private ownership and business. Both the United States and China are examples of mixed economies.

SOUTH AFRICA'S ECONOMIC SYSTEM

South Africa's economy is the most developed in Africa. As a capitalist society, it has attracted many foreign investors. Technology developed at home and imported from the West has led to South Africa's modernization. South Africa is a mixed economy that leans towards a market economy.

South African Industry

Despite being developed, South Africa's economy is still uneven. Much of the white population and a small middle class of nonwhites enjoy prosperity. However, years of apartheid's racial injustice left much of the black population in poverty and undereducated. Today, despite more freedom, many South Africans still earn low wages, lack the skills to advance to higher-paying jobs, and face high unemployment. While South Africa is more prosperous than most African nations, the percentage of citizens who enjoy its prosperity is incredibly small.

NIGERIA'S ECONOMIC SYSTEM

Nigeria's economy has improved in recent years. Increased stability has encouraged foreign investors to invest resources in the country. However, the country still suffers from severe underdevelopment. Industry is limited. Ineffective land policies, political instability, and corruption have, at times, made it difficult to attract foreign investors that might help boost the economy. Meanwhile, Nigeria is overdependent on its oil reserves for national income. When international oil prices drop,

Nigerian Poverty

Nigeria's economy experiences great difficulty. Even when oil and natural gas prices are high, government corruption often means that less than 5 percent of the nation's population actually benefits from the wealth such revenue produces.

Nigerian Stock Exchange

Although Nigeria is one of Africa's leaders in terms of agricultural output, poverty and hunger still thrive throughout the country. Despite accounting for more than 25 percent of Nigeria's revenue, Nigerian agriculture has been unable to keep pace with the country's rapidly growing population. Well over half the nation lives in extreme poverty. Agricultural mismanagement and trade policies have drained needed food supplies out of the country, increasing hunger and suffering.

Practice 3.3: Africa's Economic Systems

1. William lives in a country where the state owns most of the property and controls industrial production. William is allowed to own very little property. He also receives few if any benefits for working hard on his job. It sounds like William lives in a

   A. market economy.

   B. presidential democracy.

   C. South African city.

   D. command economy.

2. Emerson owns her own business. She owns all the equipment. She operates her business for profits. The more money the business makes, the richer Emerson gets. She bases her production on what people want to buy and what they are willing to pay. It sounds like Emerson lives in a

   A. market economy.

   B. parliamentary democracy.

   C. Nigerian city.

   D. command economy.

3. Most economic systems are

   A. command.

   B. market.

   C. mixed.

   D. democratic.

3.4 TRADE AND ECONOMIC GROWTH

TRADE

International trade occurs when nations choose to exchange goods. Nations choose to engage in trade because it is either impossible or inefficient to produce all that they need themselves. **Specialization** encourages trade. Nations specialize in producing certain products. Nigeria produces large supplies of oil. South Africa produces large amounts of diamonds. Other countries produce other products. Trade allows countries to acquire the things they need and sell the things they produce.

Trade (Cargo)

Exports are goods that a nation produces and sells to other countries. Exports bring money into the economy. **Imports** are goods that a country buys from other nations. Imports take money out of the economy.

TRADE BARRIERS

Trade barriers are obstacles to trade. Trade barriers can be natural or human-produced. Examples of **natural trade barriers** in Africa include the Sahara Desert, rainforests, mountains, and regions without access to rivers or oceans. These natural features are considered barriers because they make trade more difficult.

Atlas Mountains – Natural Trade Barrier

Political barriers are economic policies passed by a government to regulate trade. They are often intended to help a country's own producers be more competitive in the market place. At other times, they may be aimed at punishing or putting economic pressure on another country.

Sahara Desert – Natural Trade Barrier

Tariffs are taxes on imported products. Tariffs raise prices on foreign goods. This makes it less profitable for countries to sell their goods in foreign markets. Tariffs in one country normally inspire tariffs in others. For instance, if Egypt's leaders realize that their producers have to pay tariffs to trade in England, then there is a good chance that they will make English producers pay tariffs to trade in Egypt.

Quotas are limitations on the number of products that can be imported. Nations will sometimes use quotas to make products produced in their own country more competitive.

Sanctions and embargoes are other political barriers to trade. **Sanctions** are policies that restrict a country's trade with another country. They are usually meant to force a country to change some policy. **Embargoes** are even more drastic. In an embargo, nations refuse to trade with a certain country at all.

TRADE AND CURRENCY

Currency is something that is assigned value and can be used to purchase goods and services in a market. For example, in the United States, the dollar is our standard form of currency. Since countries have different forms of currency, it is important that countries understand how much their standard currency is worth in other nations. What the currency of one nation is worth in another is called the **exchange rate**.

Egyptian Pound

ECONOMIC GROWTH

FACTORS THAT CONTRIBUTE TO ECONOMIC GROWTH

Nigerian Naira

CAPITAL GOODS

Capital Goods

Several factors influence a country's **economic growth** (rate at which a country develops economically). One is its ability to invest in **capital goods**. Capital goods are goods used to produce products. Factories, machinery, the latest computers and technology, and advanced equipment are all examples of capital goods. The more modern and abundant the supply of capital goods, the more a nation can produce. The more a nation produces, the more self-sufficient it is and the more revenue it can make from foreign exports. The value of all the goods a nation produces in a year is called **gross domestic product (GDP)**. The more capital goods a nation has, the higher its GDP tends to be.

South Africa is an example of a country that has benefited from the availability of capital goods. Political instability, however, severely hurts investment in capital goods. Businesses and foreign investors don't want to invest money in markets that might change if the government is overthrown or if the nation is locked in civil war. Therefore, many African nations have a difficult time acquiring the capital goods they need for economic development.

NATURAL RESOURCES

As we have discussed, **natural resources** also affect economic development. Oil is valued worldwide. Therefore, any nation rich in oil will export large amounts that produce lots of revenue. Nations rich in other natural resources, such as valuable precious metals, will also use them to produce revenue. Diamonds, gold, and uranium are all natural resources that produce wealth and increase GDP in the nations that have them. How valued a nation's natural resources are determines how much revenue they produce and how much foreign investment they attract.

For instance, certain nations might allow foreign investors to enter their country to mine, drill, and extract certain resources in exchange for financial investments that help the country's economy. Foreign investments produce a great deal of wealth and help economies develop.

Natural Resources

HUMAN CAPITAL

Human capital refers to investments in the welfare and training of human workers. Providing for employees' health care, offering them educational opportunities, and improving their job skills through training, are all examples of investment in human capital. Investment in human capital usually produces a healthier, more satisfied, more productive workforce. More productivity results in higher GDP. More developed nations, like South Africa and Egypt, often invest more in human capital than do less-developed nations like Nigeria or Chad.

Human Capital

ENTREPRENEURS

Finally, **entrepreneurs** (people who start and own private businesses) contribute to economic development. Some nations, like Morocco, South Africa, and Kenya, encourage entrepreneurship. Others place tighter restrictions on what types of businesses may be privately owned. Usually, countries that encourage entrepreneurship have a higher GDP.

Entrepreneurs

Practice 3.4: Trade and Economic Growth

1. When nations exchange goods, it is called
   A. international tariff.
   B. international trade.
   C. international capital.
   D. entrepreneurship.

2. What is GDP?

3. What are capital goods, natural resources, and human capital? How do they affect GDP?

CHAPTER 3 REVIEW

Key Terms

unitary government
confederation
federation
autocracy
oligarchy
democracy
parliamentary democracy
prime minister
presidential democracy
president
Kenya's government
South Africa's government
Sudan's government
education in Sudan
education in Kenya
civil wars
four factors that lead to conflicts and civil wars
refugees
famines
AIDS
economics
three basic economic questions
traditional economies
command economies

market economies
capitalism
market
mixed economies
South Africa's economy
Nigeria's economy
international trade
specialization
exports
imports
trade barriers
natural trade barriers
political trade barriers
tariffs
quotas
sanctions
embargoes
currency
exchange rate
economic growth
capital goods
gross domestic product (GDP)
natural resources
human capital
entrepreneurs

Chapter Review Questions:

1. South Africa's government is **best** described as a
   A. mixed economy.
   B. democracy.
   C. autocracy.
   D. oligarchy.

2. Which of the following countries has an autocratic government?
   A. South Africa
   B. Egypt
   C. Kenya
   D. Sudan

3. Uchena lives in a nation in which rival ethnic groups are fighting a bloody war. They are fighting over who will run the government and control the nation's natural resources. Uchena's country is experiencing
   A. famine.
   B. economic growth.
   C. civil war.
   D. a market economy.

4. In which country does the legislature have the **most** power?

   A. South Africa

   B. Kenya

   C. Sudan

   D. The legislature has very little power in each of these countries.

5. When nations limit trade with a country in an effort to get it to change its policies, it is known as

   A. sanctions.

   B. embargoes.

   C. tariffs.

   D. autocracy.

6. When nations refuse to trade with a nation at all, it is called a/an

   A. tariff.

   B. capitalism.

   C. command economy.

   D. embargo.

NATION	CURRENCY	EXCHANGE RATE AGAINST THE DOLLAR
Egypt	Egyptian Pound (£)	5.97
South Africa	Rand (R)	8.02
Nigeria	Naira (₦)	136.00
Chad	CFA Franc (FCFA)	560.00

7. Bill is a U.S. citizen. He lives in the state of Georgia. He wants to visit a country where his U.S. dollar will have the greatest value. According to the chart above, in which country would Bill's dollar buy the **most** goods and services?

   A. Egypt

   B. Nigeria

   C. Chad

   D. South Africa

8. Use the same chart you did in #7. Based on the chart, in which nation would Egypt's currency carry the **least** value?

   A. Chad

   B. South Africa

   C. Nigeria

   D. One cannot tell based on the chart.

9. An economic system in which property is privately owned, there is little government regulation, and the market determines production is called a
   A. command economy.
   B. market economy.
   C. parliamentary democracy.
   D. oligarchy.

10. An economic system in which the government owns property and sets production is called a
    A. command economy.
    B. state economy.
    C. governmental economy.
    D. market economy.

11. When a country invests in technology, builds factories, and imports the latest machines, it is an investment in
    A. human capital.
    B. natural resources.
    C. education.
    D. capital goods.

12. People who help boost economic development by starting businesses are called
    A. autocrats.
    B. economists.
    C. entrepreneurs.
    D. human capitalists.

Chapter 4
Geographic Understandings of Southwest Asia

This chapter covers the following Georgia standards.

SS7G5	The student will locate selected features in Southwestern Asia (Middle East).
SS7G6	The student will discuss environmental issues across Southwest Asia (Middle East).
SS7G7	The student will explain the impact of location, climate, physical characteristics, distribution of natural resources and population distribution on Southwest Asia (Middle East).
SS7G8	The student will describe the diverse cultures of the people who live in Southwest Asia (Middle East).

4.1 PHYSICAL FEATURES AND NATIONS OF SOUTHWEST ASIA

NATIONS OF SOUTHWEST ASIA

ISRAEL

Israel sits at the crossroad between Asia and Africa. Its location has long made Israel a coveted territory. Traders and armies traveling over land back and forth between Asia and Africa have

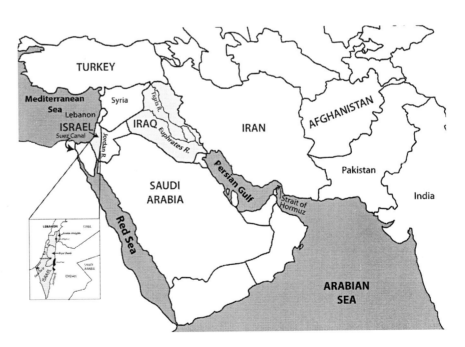

Nations of Southwest Asia

had to go through what is today Israel. For this reason, empires and nations throughout history have sought to control the territory.

Israel also possesses several **occupied territories**. These are areas taken from Arab nations following a war. In the north, Israel occupies the Golan Heights. The Golan Heights allow Israel to control crucial high ground from which they can defend against an attack from their northern enemy, Syria.

Occupied Territories

In addition to the Golan Heights, Israel also occupies the West Bank (territory along the west bank of the Jordan River) and East Jerusalem. The Sinai Peninsula was once one of the occupied areas as well, but Israel returned it to Egypt as part of a peace agreement.

Today, the occupied territories cause great tension between Arabs and Israelis. Arabs claim that these territories should be returned to Arab peoples. Israelis, however, argue that Israel won them as the result of defending itself against Arab attacks. As Israeli settlers move into these areas, Arabs often respond with violent protests. In recent years, Israel has slowed development of Israeli settlements and, at times, tried to move Israelis out of the occupied territories in an effort to improve Palestinian relations. Such moves, however, have done little to calm the Arab-Israeli conflict and invite anger and resistance from Zionist Jews.

Israel is also home to the city of **Jerusalem**. An ancient city, Jerusalem is sacred to Jews, Christians, and Muslims. It is the city where King Solomon built the first Jewish temple. It is where Jesus was crucified and where his followers claim he rose from the dead. Muslims recognize Jerusalem as the place from which Muhammad ascended to heaven.

Jerusalem

For centuries, Christians and Muslims fought for control of the holy city during a period called the Crusades. During other times, Christians, Jews, and Muslims shared the city peacefully. In 1948, Israel took charge of West Jerusalem after it became an independent nation. East Jerusalem remained part of Arab Palestine. Israel occupied East Jerusalem as part of the Six-Day War and has controlled the entire city ever since.

Palestinian People in Gaza Strip

THE GAZA STRIP

Israel also oversees an area along the Mediterranean coast between Israel and Egypt known as the **Gaza Strip**. Intense conflict exists in Gaza. Most of the people who live there are Palestinians. They resent Israel.

For thirty-eight years, Israel's military occupied the region. In 2005, the Israelis pulled out. Since then, radical Palestinian groups have used Gaza to launch attacks against Israel. At the same time, Israel has often been accused of striking back at Gaza with little concern for the innocent civilians who live there. In early 2008, Israel cut off much of Gaza's access to fuel and electricity in an effort to end Palestinian military strikes. Critics claimed Israel's actions were a violation of international law that harmed innocent civilians. Palestinians in the Gaza Strip destroyed portions of the fence separating Gaza from Egypt so that refugees could escape across the border in search of needed supplies.

Fighting between Palestinians and Israel

SAUDI ARABIA

The kingdom of **Saudi Arabia** occupies most of the Arabian Peninsula. Saudi Arabia exports more oil than any other nation on earth. Oil accounts for over two-thirds of the Saudi government's revenue. Saudi Arabia is also the home of Mecca and Medina, the two holiest cities in Islam. The Red Sea is to the west of Saudi Arabia, and the Persian Gulf is to the east.

King Abdullah bin Abdul Aziz Al Saud of Saudia Arabia

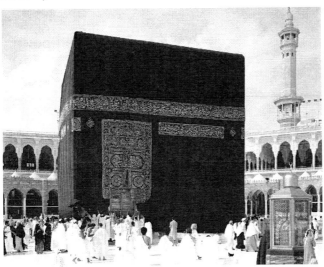

Mecca

Saudi Arabia has a diverse geography. Mountain ranges run along the western portion of the country. The plateau of Nejd covers much of the nation's center. In the east, rocky and sandy lowlands run all the way to the Persian Gulf shore. Much of southern Saudi Arabia is covered by dry, harsh desert. However, parts of the southwest feature mountain areas with cooler temperatures. The climate is extremely hot and dry. Summer temperatures regularly top 120°F. Winter temperatures usually average around 50°F in the country's coldest regions.

Saudi Arabia is a Muslim state. The Qur'an (Islam's holy book), other Muslim writings, and generations of tradition combine to form Saudi Arabia's laws. These laws greatly restrict women's rights. They limit how women may dress and act in public. The Saudis also practice a strict legal code. In some cases, the state will beat offenders or cut off their hands or feet for crimes like stealing. Following a judicial process, serious crimes often carry the death penalty.

Most Saudis are Arabs. Over two hundred thousand Palestinians live in Saudi Arabia as well. However, like many other Arab states, Saudi Arabia will not grant these Palestinians citizenship for fear that it will lead to the loss of Palestinian identity and the end of anti-Israeli resistance. Saudi Arabia also hosts many foreign workers, particularly in its oil industry.

IRAQ

Iraq lies east of Syria, Jordan, and Saudi Arabia. It sits west of Iran. Iraq covers a region often referred to as the "cradle of civilization." Its capital is Baghdad, one of the most glorious cities in history. The country is mostly desert. However, two of the world's oldest and most important rivers run through the country: the **Tigris River** and the **Euphrates River**. The Tigris runs south out of Turkey and past Baghdad before eventually meeting the Euphrates and emptying into the Persian Gulf. The Euphrates flows south through Syria and Iraq. Both provide fertile farmland and water supplies.

Euphrates River

Mountains cover most of northern Iraq. Winters are mild and cool through much of the country, with summers being extremely hot and dry. In the higher mountain elevations, cold winter temperatures produce snowfalls that can cause flooding when the warm months return. Like Saudi Arabia, Iraq has abundant oil and natural gas reserves. Experts estimate that close to 90 percent of Iraq's oil is yet to be extracted for use.

Baghdad

IRAN

Once known as Persia, **Iran** sits at the heart of the Persian Gulf region. It is one of the largest countries in Southwest Asia. Persian (also called Farsi) is the official language, rather than Arabic.

Various ethnic groups call Iran home. Azeris, Turks, Kurds, Arabs, and Persians are just a few of the people groups that populate Iran. Historically, Iran is home to the world's oldest civilizations. Some date back as far as 4000 BC. Oil is abundant and serves as Iran's major source of income.

Child from Iran

Most of Iran sits in the Iranian plateau. It is a very mountainous country, with most of the population living in the west. To the east lie desert regions. They remain dry because the western mountains prevent moisture from reaching them.

AFGHANISTAN

Afghanistan sits directly east of Iran. It sits at the crossroad of eastern and western Asia. It has historically been an important area for trade and is home to a diverse population. It is extremely mountainous, borders no bodies of water, and is very dry. Summers are very hot, and winters are very cold. Because of its location, the nation is also susceptible to earthquakes.

Afghanistan

TURKEY

Turkey covers the Anatolian Peninsula in Southwest Asia. It lies at the crossroad of Europe and Asia. The modern Republic of Turkey was founded after WWI and the fall of the Ottoman Empire (the Ottoman Empire will be discussed in chapter 5).

PHYSICAL FEATURES

IMPORTANT BODIES OF WATER

Southwest Asia is home to a number of important rivers. As mentioned earlier, the Tigris and Euphrates run through Iraq. The **Jordan River** runs along the border between Jordan and Israel. It divides the two countries. The Jordan is considered a sacred river. Jews believe it is the river Joshua crossed when he first led the Jewish people into Palestine thousands of years ago. Christians recognize it as the river in which Jesus was baptized.

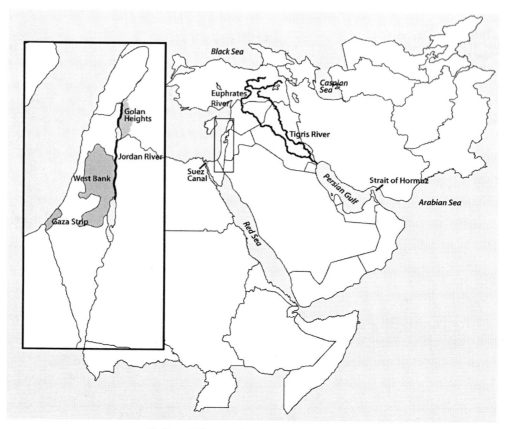

Bodies of Water in Southwest Asia

There are other important bodies of water in Southwest Asia as well. The **Suez Canal** is a man-made waterway across part of Egypt. It connects the Mediterranean Sea and the Red Sea. The Suez Canal allows ships to travel back and forth between the two bodies of water without having to travel around Africa.

The **Red Sea** sits between North Africa and the Arabian Peninsula's western shore. It has long allowed Asia and Africa to engage in trade with one another by water, while providing countries like Egypt access to the Indian Ocean.

The **Persian Gulf** separates the eastern shore of the Arabian Peninsula and Iran. Nations around the world recognize its importance to the world economy. It provides trading access for the abundant oil exports from Iran and the Arabian Peninsula. However, its importance also makes it an area where many wars are fought.

Ships in the Persian Gulf

The **Strait of Hormuz** is a narrow strait that connects the Persian Gulf to the **Arabian Sea**. The Arabian Sea leads to the Indian Ocean and important ocean trade routes. Because of its importance, nations have often been willing to go to war to keep the Strait of Hormuz open.

Practice 4.1: Physical Features and Nations of SW Asia

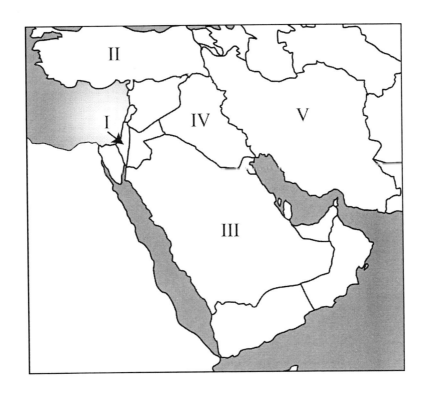

1. Which country on the map above is home to Jerusalem and the occupied territories?

   A. I

   B. II

   C. III

   D. IV

2. Saudi Arabia covers most of the

   A. Anatolian Peninsula.

   B. Persian Gulf.

   C. Arabian Peninsula.

   D. Gaza Strip.

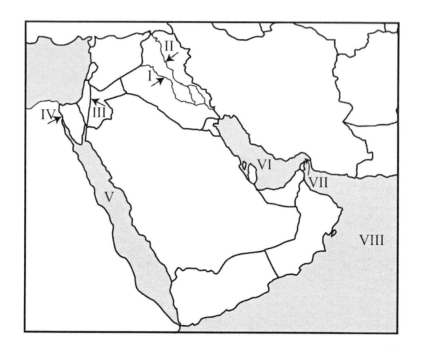

3. The following bodies of water are shown on the map above. Write each one beside the correct corresponding Roman numeral.

Persian Gulf   Suez Canal

Arabian Sea   Red Sea

Strait of Hormuz   Jordan River

Tigris River   Euphrates River

I _____   V _____

II _____   VI _____

III _____   VII _____

IV _____   VIII _____

4.2 ENVIRONMENTAL ISSUES AND THE IMPACT OF CLIMATE

Southwest Asia is a diverse region with different climates. Much of the region is desert and not very inhabitable. Nations like Turkey, Iran, and Afghanistan are very mountainous with higher elevations that are cooler and sometimes even receive snowfall. Parts of Syria, Lebanon, and Israel are very fertile and enjoy the milder climate of the Mediterranean coast. The Arabian Peninsula regularly reaches temperatures around 120°F during the summers. Like other areas of the world, people who live in Southwest Asia adapt their lifestyles to the kind of climate in which they live.

WATER AND AGRICULTURE

THE IMPORTANCE OF WATER

Almost all of Southwest Asia is dry. As a result, **water** is incredibly important. Water is necessary for people and animals to live and for crops to grow. Therefore, most people live close to water supplies, such as along rivers or in urban areas. In small, rural settlements, maintaining clean and functioning wells is very important because very little rain falls during the year.

Oasis

AGRICULTURE

Southwest Asia's climate also affects **agriculture** (farming). Farmers live in limited fertile regions or grow crops that need less water. Farmers often plant close to rivers where the water nourishes the soil and can be used for irrigation. Oases and underground water supplies also allow people to farm.

In nations like Saudi Arabia, Kuwait, Israel, and Lebanon, where economies are more developed or the nation depends heavily on oil, agriculture does not produce as much revenue. In less-developed regions, such as Afghanistan, agriculture plays a bigger role. Agriculture remains a major source of survival for people in rural areas.

Southwest Asia Farming

In an effort to grow more food, nations like Saudi Arabia have invested in **desalinization**. It is a process that removes salt from sea water. Since areas like the Arabian Peninsula are surrounded by salt water, desalinization greatly increases the amount of usable water.

Many nations also rely on irrigation. **Irrigation** is a method used by farmers. It is a process by which water is transported from rivers, lakes, or other water supplies, to farms. Irrigation allows farmers to grow crops in areas that would normally be unsuitable for farming.

ENVIRONMENTAL ISSUES

WATER POLLUTION

Countries in Southwest Asia face **environmental issues**. Millions of people rely on the same rivers and sources of water for survival. Rivers like the Jordan, Tigris, and Euphrates provide needed water to more than one country. Therefore, **water pollution** is a major concern in the Middle East.

As nations strive to develop and grow their economics, they try to attract more business and industrialization. However, industrialization also creates more pollutants, affecting the quality of air and water.

Life Along Major Southwest Asia Rivers

People also pay close attention to **water rights**. Since different regions rely on the same water supplies, disputes often arise. When Turkey builds a dam on the Tigris River, it affects Iraq farther south. Israel and Jordan often have conflicts regarding the Jordan River.

Growing cities and increasing populations put additional strain on limited water supplies. In rural areas, locals still feud over well rights. These are just a few examples of water-related issues that exist in the Middle East.

THE IMPACT OF OIL

Extraction also affects the environment. Drilling for oil and mining precious metals takes a toll on the landscape. The methods used to extract such resources often leave the land damaged and unusable.

The **distribution of oil** in Southwest Asia has consequences. Nations with rich oil supplies rely heavily on them for revenue. Some countries, like Saudi Arabia and Kuwait, have grown very wealthy as a result. Other nations that lack oil, such as Turkey, Israel, and Afghanistan, have had to find other sources of revenue. Due to their relatively free economies, Turkey and Israel have managed to thrive. Meanwhile, Afghanistan has suffered as an underdeveloped nation, due to a more restrictive economy.

Southwest Asia Oil Fields

Practice 4.2: Environmental Issues and the Impact of Climate

1. Why do most people in Southwest Asia tend to live close to rivers or in urban areas with modern infrastructure?

    A. Much of Southwest Asia is very dry and these areas offer needed access to water supplies.

    B. There are fewer environmental issues in urban areas, and water is not an environmental concern.

    C. There is less need for fresh water in these areas.

    D. Most people live in desert regions or in mountainous regions, not near rivers or in urban areas.

2. How does the distribution of oil affect nations in Southwest Asia?

4.3 PEOPLES OF SOUTHWEST ASIA

JEWS

Many nations and peoples make up the Middle East. Many **Jews** live in Israel, which was founded as a Jewish state in 1948. Their claim to parts of Palestine is based on the fact that it was once home to the ancient nation of Israel. Today, generations of Jews have grown up living their whole lives in modern Israel.

Israeli Jews

ARABS

Much of Southwest Asia's population is Arab. **Arabs** are people who can trace their ancestors to the original tribes of Arabia. Arab peoples have lived in the Middle East for thousands of years. Their predominant language is Arabic. Most Arabs are Muslims; however, many are Christians or hold to other faiths. Lebanon, Syria, Jordan, Iraq, and the Arabian Peninsula all feature large Arab populations. As we have discussed, Palestinians within Israeli-controlled areas are predominantly Arabs as well.

Palestinian Arab

KURDS

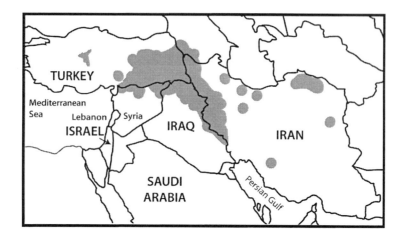

The **Kurds** are an ethnic group found in parts of Iran, Iraq, Syria, Turkey, Armenia, Azerbaijan, and Lebanon. They originate from an area often referred to as Kurdistan. They speak Kurdish and are often the victims of discrimination.

Kurds have long called for an independent Kurdistan to be carved out of portions of the countries in which Kurdish peoples live. For years, some Kurdish groups have launched military campaigns in their quest for independence.

Kurd

PERSIANS

Persians originate from Iran and still live in the regions around the Persian Gulf. While most Persians live in Iran, some also live in surrounding countries. The majority of Persians are Shia Muslims. (See section on the differences between Sunni and Shia Muslims later in this chapter).

RELIGIONS OF SOUTHWEST ASIA

There are a number of different religious groups in Southwest Asia. (Review chapter 1, section 1.3, regarding the difference between ethnic groups and religious groups.)

JUDAISM

Judaism traces its origins to the prophet Abraham. It teaches that there is one God and that the Jewish people are His chosen nation. Judaism is the official religion of Israel. Jewish people rely on the Tanakh (Jewish holy scriptures) and Talmud (Jewish writings) to provide religious direction on how to live a life that honors God.

Jews at the Wailing Wall

CHRISTIANITY

Christianity arose out of Judaism. During the first century, a Jewish teacher named Jesus claimed to be the son of God. Roman officials ultimately executed him in Jerusalem. Jesus' followers claim that he died to pay for the sins of mankind, and that he rose from the dead after three days. They believe that faith in Jesus and holding to his teachings are the keys to eternal life. Many Southwest Asian nations have sizeable Christian populations.

A Lebanese Christian

ISLAM

The most popular faith in Southwest Asia is **Islam**. The prophet **Muhammad** founded Islam after claiming to be visited by an angel. Followers of Islam believe in the same God as Jews and Christians. They refer to God as **Allah**. However, they believe that Muhammad's teachings and the **Qur'an** (Islam's holy book) hold God's true message. The religion requires that **Muslims** (followers of Islam) hold to the **Five Pillars of Islam**. These pillars are:

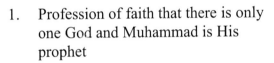
Southwest Asia Muslims in Prayer

1. Profession of faith that there is only one God and Muhammad is His prophet

2. Prayer five times a day

3. Giving alms to the poor

4. Fasting during Ramadan (a holy month in the Muslim calendar)

5. The Hajj (a holy pilgrimage to Mecca—Muhammad's birthplace—that every Muslim is supposed to take at least once).

The Hajj

DIVISIONS IN ISLAM

After Muhammad's death in 632 AD, major disagreements arose in Islam. Muslims had different opinions over who should lead the religion. Two main factions formed. **Sunni** Muslims do not believe that *caliphs* (leaders of Islam) have to be blood descendants of

Muhammad. **Shia** Muslims believe that only blood relatives of the prophet have a right to lead. Shias acknowledge Muhammad's cousin and son-in-law, Ali ibn Abi Talib, as the first true *Imam* (spiritual leader). They believe that the Imam is granted authority directly by Allah.

Mecca, Saudi Arabia

Sunnis and Shias disagree over interpretations of Muslim teachings as well. Today, Sunnis make up the largest number of Muslims in the world and Shias the second largest. Historically, relations between the two have often been violent.

LITERACY

Countries depend on education. A strong educational system equips people to pursue economic, political, and social development. A country's educational system can be judged, in part, by its literacy rate. **Literacy** refers to a person's ability to read and write.

In parts of Southwest Asia, education has long been an important part of the culture (the oldest university in the world is in Yemen). Some areas, however, have fallen behind in modern times. Many Southwest Asian nations did not officially become independent countries until the mid-twentieth century. As a result, their educational systems are less than eighty years old.

Education in Southwest Asia

Despite some nations' late start, most of Southwest Asia is advancing in education. Israel's high literacy rate has helped it to become the most economically developed nation in the Middle East. Syria enjoys a literacy rate of over 80 percent for males and over 70 percent for females. Iran also enjoys a nationwide literacy rate of almost 80 percent.

Saudi Arabia became a country in 1932. Because it is based on strict Muslim law, it did not originally grant women the same educational opportunities as men. Today, however, Saudi Arabia offers a free education to all citizens. The government devotes over 25% of its annual budget to supporting schools and universities. Although it finances the study of traditional arts and sciences, the study of Islam remains the foundation of Saudi Arabia's educational system.

Practice 4.3: Peoples of Southwest Asia

1. Describe Arab peoples.

2. Describe Persian peoples.

3. Describe the Kurds.

4. Describe the differences between Shia and Sunni Muslims.

CHAPTER 4 REVIEW

Key Terms

Israel
occupied territories
Jerusalem
Gaza Strip
Saudi Arabia
Iraq
Tigris River
Euphrates River
Iran
Afghanistan
Turkey
Jordan River
Suez Canal
Red Sea
Persian Gulf
Strait of Hormuz
Arabian Sea
importance of water
agriculture
desalinization
irrigation

environmental issues
water pollution
water rights
extraction
distribution of oil
Jews
Arabs
Kurds
Persians
Judaism
Christianity
Islam
Muhammad
Allah
Qur'an
Muslims
Five Pillars of Islam
Sunni Muslims
Shia Muslims
literacy

Chapter Review Questions

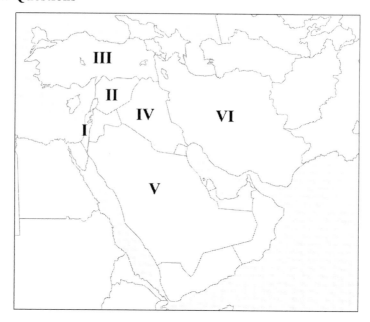

1. In which of the following nations would one expect to find the greatest amount of conflict between Israelis and Palestinians?

   A. I   B. II   C. VI   D. V

2. Using the same map from question #1, in which of the following countries would one expect to find a society based on strict Muslim law?

   A. I   C. V

   B. III   D. I and II

3. Which of the following is included among the Occupied Territories?

   A. West Jerusalem

   B. the Negev

   C. Jordan

   D. the Golan Heights

4. The Occupied Territories are

   A. areas of the Arabian Peninsula that have enough fertile land to support human life.

   B. parts of Southwest Asia with enough water to support stable populations.

   C. areas that belonged to Arabs that are currently occupied by the nation of Israel.

   D. territories given to Israel that have since been conquered by Arabs.

5. One would expect to find the greatest number of Persians in
   A. Iran.
   B. Iraq.
   C. Saudi Arabia.
   D. Israel.

Look at the map below, and answer the following question.

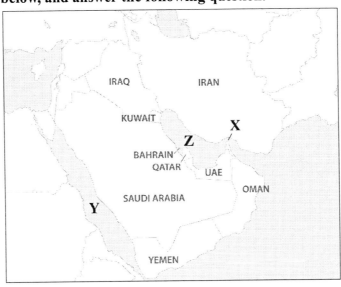

6. Which of the following is accurate?
   A. X denotes the Red Sea.
   B. Y denotes the Red Sea.
   C. Z denotes the Strait of Hormuz.
   D. Y denotes the Persian Gulf.

7. Using the same map as #6, which of the following denotes a key passage connecting the Persian Gulf to the Arabian Sea?
   A. X
   B. Y
   C. Z
   D. none

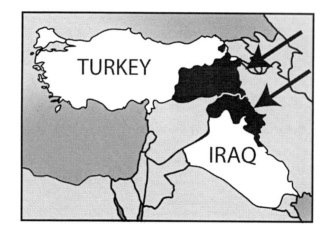

8. Look at the map above. Which people group occupies this area in large numbers?
   A. Persians

   B. Jews

   C. Kurds

   D. Saudis

9. Islam is a religion founded by
   A. Muhammad.

   B. Muslims.

   C. the Qur'an.

   D. the Hajj.

Chapter 5
Historical Understandings of Southwest Asia

This chapter covers the following Georgia standard.

SS7H2	The student will analyze continuity and change in Southwest Asia (Middle East) leading to the 21st century.

5.1 SOUTHWEST ASIA BEFORE EUROPEAN PARTITIONING

THE REGION AND RELIGION

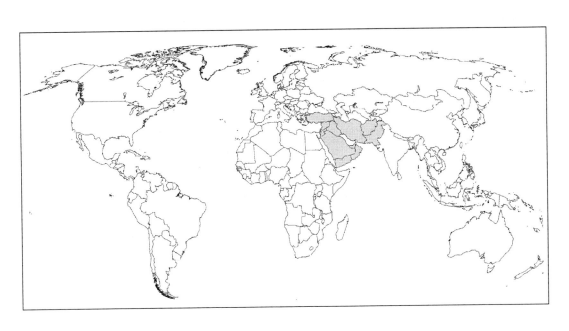

The shaded region on the map above is **Southwest Asia**. Many people refer to this region as the Middle East (scholars often refer to it as the *Near East*). For centuries, kingdoms and empires have battled for control of Southwest Asia.

One reason is its location. Southwest Asia lies at the meeting point of three continents (Europe, Africa, and Asia). Important trade routes have long passed through the region. For many years, whoever controlled Southwest Asia held great influence over much of the world's economy.

JUDAISM

Three of the world's major religions originated in Southwest Asia: Judaism, Christianity, and Islam. All three faiths trace their ancestry back thousands of years to the prophet **Abraham**. According to the book of Genesis (first book of the Old Testament of the Bible), Abraham traveled from the land of Ur (modern-day Iraq) to Palestine (modern-day Israel) following a command from God.

Abraham

Followers of **Judaism** recognize Abraham as the father of their faith. They believe that there is only one God. The Jewish scriptures teach that God promised Abraham the land of Palestine for him and his descendants. As descendants of Abraham, Jews believe that they are God's chosen people. They hold that they are the ones entitled to the land God promised Abraham. Today, the modern state of Israel exists as a Jewish state in Palestine.

CHRISTIANITY

Around the beginning of the first century, a Jewish teacher named **Jesus** founded **Christianity**. According to many first century writers, Jesus claimed to be the promised Messiah (savior of the Jewish people) and the son of God. His followers believe that when he was crucified by the Roman government, he was actually dying to pay for humankind's sins. His disciples claimed that, after three days, he arose from the dead and ascended to heaven.

Early Christianity

After Jesus' death, his followers quickly spread Christianity to parts of Asia, North Africa, and Europe. Teaching that the only way to know God and find salvation is through faith in Jesus, they challenged many of the pagan religions throughout the world.

Today, large Christian communities continue to exist in Southwest Asia. Lebanon, Egypt, Israel, and Syria all boast large Christian populations.

ISLAM

Islam emerged in the seventh century. Claiming that an angel had come to him and revealed God's will, the prophet **Muhammad** preached that there is only one God: **Allah**. He taught that Abraham, Moses, and Jesus were each prophets, but that Jews and Christians had misunderstood their teachings.

Early Islam

Many of the poor who heard Muhammad's message accepted it because he called for social justice and equality. A great number of powerful leaders and rich merchants, however, rejected Muhammad. They saw him as a threat to their economic security. In 622 AD, Muhammad and his followers fled their hometown of Mecca and settled in Medina. Muslims (followers of Islam) recognize this as the first year of the Muslim calendar and the official beginning of Islam. Eventually, Muhammad's enemies followed him to Medina in hopes of destroying his religion forever.

Qur'an

Muhammad's forces defeated them, however, and soon converted most of Arabia to Islam. Some of Muhammad's followers eventually wrote down his revelations in the **Qur'an** (Islam's holy book).

Within a century, Islam spread throughout Southwest Asia and North Africa. Muslims even conquered parts of Spain. Their military campaigns were inspired both by a desire to spread Islam and, for some, a desire for wealth and power.

THE OTTOMAN EMPIRE

A number of Islamic empires eventually rose to power. The greatest and longest lasting was the **Ottoman Empire**. It started during the fourteenth century when a leader named Osman I united a number of individual chiefdoms in Anatolia (modern-day Turkey). Through successful military campaigns and the promise of booty (wealth taken after battle), Osman gained soldiers and his domain grew.

During the century following Osman's death, the Ottoman Empire spread. From 1453 through the sixteenth century, the Ottomans continued to expand and conquer new lands. Their empire spread into Europe, North Africa, and further east into Asia. Over time the Ottoman Empire weakened as different territories demanded and won independence. Still, the empire lasted into the early twentieth century.

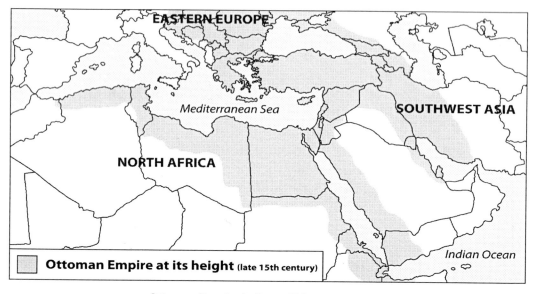

Ottoman Empire in Later Fifteenth Century

EUROPEAN PARTITIONING OF SOUTHWEST ASIA

A series of wars during the early twentieth century ended the Ottoman Empire. Italy seized control of Libya in North Africa as a result of the Italo-Turkish War of 1911. The Balkan Wars (1912–1913) resulted in the loss of the last of the Ottomans' Balkan territories. Finally, as an ally of Germany and Austria-Hungary, the Ottoman Empire found itself on the losing side in World War I. The peace treaty ending the war divided the empire and ceded many of its territories to the victorious European powers. Under the **mandate system**, Southwest Asia was partitioned (divided) between France and Great Britain.

Osman I

The mandate system left Arabs bitter. Many of them helped defeat the Ottomans and thought that the victorious European nations would reward them with independence after the war.

Partitioning also created **artificial boundaries**. European leaders divided the region based on resources and coveted territories, not based on Southwest Asian history or ethnic groups. Some ethnic groups were divided. Others were left without any land to call their own. To this day, violent conflicts continue as different people groups try to claim land they believe was unjustly taken from them by European colonizers and the mandate system.

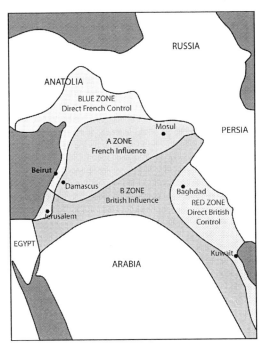

Southwest Asian Boundaries as a Result of WWI's Mandate System

Practice 5.1:   Southwest Asia before European Partitioning

1. Islam was founded by

   A. Abraham.   B. Jesus.   C. Muhammad.   D. Osman I.

2. What was the mandate system, and how did it affect Southwest Asia?

5.2 ISRAEL AND THE ARAB WORLD

ANTI-SEMITISM IN EUROPE

Anti-Semitism (racism against Jewish people) existed in Europe for hundreds of years before the nineteenth century. During the 1800s it became more intense. Of all the nations in Europe, Germany showed the most tolerance. As a result, many Jews migrated to Germany and the country's Jewish population quickly grew. A great number of Jews eventually owned businesses and played important roles in Germany's economic and political system.

Jews in a Concentration Camp during the Holocaust

Things began to change after Germany's defeat in World War I. The Allies who had fought against Germany forced the Germans to sign a humiliating treaty. Germany had to accept full blame for the war, seriously decrease their military, and pay reparations (money a losing nation pays to a victorious nation after a war to cover the cost of the war's destruction). The harsh sanctions made Germans very bitter and caused incredible economic hardship. Germans began looking for someone to blame. A young, charismatic leader by the name of Adolf Hitler took advantage of this discontent. As head of the Nazi Party, Hitler gained political popularity by promising to restore the glory of Germany and blaming the Jews for the country's hardship.

Adolf Hitler

In 1933, Hitler became Germany's leader. Following Hitler's orders, German forces invaded Poland in 1939, officially beginning World War II. When the Allies (the nations that fought against Germany) finally defeated Germany in 1945, the world learned that something horrifying had been taking place inside Nazi territories. Hitler had launched a plan meant to totally destroy the Jewish people. Under the Nazis, more than six million people, most of them Jews, were executed or died after enduring torture and starvation in concentration camps. Many others suffered in these camps until Allied forces finally liberated them. This terrible period became known as **the Holocaust**.

Nuremberg Trial of Nazi Leaders Responsible for the Holocaust

ZIONISM AND THE MODERN STATE OF ISRAEL

From 1922 to 1948, Great Britain controlled **Palestine** as part of the mandate system. During this same era, **Zionism** (Jewish nationalism) gained momentum in Europe. Zionists wanted Palestine to become home to an independent Jewish state.

After the Holocaust, support for the Zionist cause increased. In addition, Great Britain had grown weary of overseeing Palestine. In 1947, it handed control of Palestine over to the United Nations (an international organization established after WWII that is devoted to maintaining peace). In 1948, the United Nations formally recognized the modern state of **Israel** and granted the nation control over formerly British Palestine.

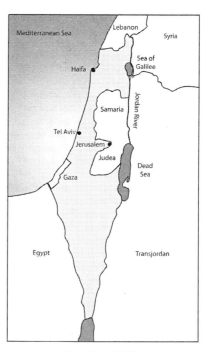

Israel in 1948

ARAB-ISRAELI CONFLICT

Not everyone welcomed the new Jewish nation. **Arabs** across the Middle East responded with outrage. They viewed Palestine as belonging to Arab **Palestinians** and felt that Palestine should have become an independent Arab state after WWI. The creation of Israel led to the removal of more than three million Palestinians who were forced to leave their homes and relocate to refugee camps. Since 1948, Arabs and Israelis have battled consistently over Palestine.

Leaders in the Six-Day War

SOUTHWEST ASIAN WARS

Numerous wars have been fought between Israel and Arab nations. In 1956, Israeli forces invaded the Sinai Peninsula after Egypt attempted to block an Israeli port. Despite their success and the support of British and French troops, the Israelis withdrew under pressure from the United States and Soviet Union.

Eleven years later, Egypt, Syria, and Jordan went to war with Israel in the Six-Day War. Although their enemies enjoyed the support of the Arab world, Israel won the brief conflict, seizing the Sinai Peninsula, the Gaza Strip, the West Bank, East Jerusalem, and the Golan Heights. To this day, control of these areas is a source of conflict and bitterness between Israelis and Arabs.

In 1973, Egypt and Syria led Arab states in launching a surprise attack against Israel. It became known as the Yom Kippur War because the attack occurred on the Jewish holy day of Yom Kippur. At first the Arabs made great advances into Israeli territory. However, by the time the United Nations intervened to negotiate a cease-fire, the momentum had shifted to Israel.

Israeli Soldiers

RELIGIOUS CONFLICT

Land is not the only source of conflict in Southwest Asia. **Religious conflict** also occurs. Islam is the most popular religion in Southwest Asia. Arabs, Persians, and other people groups boast large Muslim populations (although, not all members of these people groups are Muslims). Most Israelis are Jewish. Large Christian populations exist in a number of countries as well. Some of the bitterness that exists in Southwest Asia is due to religious differences as well as conflicts over land.

Muslim Fighter

Practice 5.2: Israel and the Arab World

1. What was the Holocaust? How did it contribute to the founding of the modern state of Israel?

2. Who of the following were supportive of the founding of the modern state of Israel?
   A. Zionists

   B. Arabs

   C. Palestinians

   D. anti-Semites

5.3 U.S. INVOLVEMENT IN SOUTHWEST ASIA

IMPACT OF THE COLD WAR

The United States has remained very involved in Southwest Asia since World War II. After the war, the United States and the Soviet Union entered a period known as the **cold war**. Although the two countries worked together to defeat Germany, they did not trust each other. The Soviet Union was a communist nation with a command economy. The United States was a free democracy with a mixed-market economy. The United States was determined to prevent Soviet-backed communism from spreading into Southwest Asia. Over time, the United States became Israel's ally. The Soviet Union became an ally to many Arab nations.

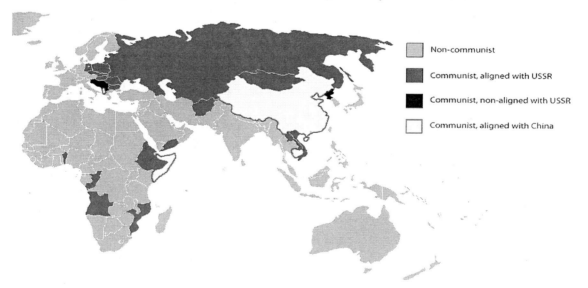

Africa and Asia Loyalties during the Cold War

THE GULF WAR

In August 1990, Iraq invaded the small Persian Gulf nation of Kuwait. Iraqi President **Saddam Hussein** claimed the territory rightfully belonged to Iraq. He also wanted Kuwait's rich oil fields. Kuwait and neighboring Saudi Arabia were important sources of oil for the United States. This made the invasion particularly disturbing for the United States. U.S. President George H.W. Bush worked through the UN to form an alliance of countries against Iraq. When Saddam refused to withdraw from Kuwait, the U.S.-led alliance invaded the territory. The **Gulf War** lasted just forty-two days and resulted in the liberation of Kuwait. Saddam Hussein, however, remained in power.

Saddam Hussein

Gulf War

AFGHANISTAN, IRAQ, AND THE WAR ON TERROR

SEPTEMBER 11, 2001

On **September 11, 2001,** Muslim terrorists from Southwest Asia hijacked four U.S. airliners. They flew two of them into the twin towers of the World Trade Center in New York City. The massive towers came crashing down, killing thousands. Meanwhile, in Washington, D.C., terrorists flew a third plane into the Pentagon (the center of U.S. military command). The fourth and final plane went down in a Pennsylvania field. Most believe it was bound for either the Capitol or the White House. The passengers on board revolted against the hijackers, causing the plane to crash instead, killing everyone on board. The 9/11 attacks left U.S. citizens across the nation shocked and saddened.

9/11 Attacks

THE WAR ON TERROR

The terrorist group, **al Qaeda**, carried out the 9/11 attacks. **Osama bin Laden** leads al-Qaeda and was the mastermind behind the attacks. Al-Qaeda began as a resistance movement against the Soviet invasion of Afghanistan during the late '70s and early '80s. However, once the Soviets withdrew, the group turned its focus to advancing a radical form of Islam. Al Qaeda's interpretation of Islam calls for expelling foreigners from the holy lands (Middle East). It also seeks to overthrow what it views as corrupt regimes in Southwest Asia. To accomplish these goals, al Qaeda also calls for the destruction of any state it feels props up these regimes. Among the nations it hopes to destroy are Israel, the United States, and other Western powers.

Osama bin Laden

As a response to 9/11, President George W. Bush (the oldest son of President George H.W. Bush) declared a U.S. **War on Terror**. Bush vowed that the United States would go after foreign terrorists rather than waiting for them to attack again. He assembled an international coalition (alliance) that invaded **Afghanistan** in October 2001. The U.S.-led force quickly toppled the Taliban government that offered a safe haven to bin Laden. Bin Laden, meanwhile, went into hiding. Many believe he fled to neighboring Pakistan, where he would have found many people

War in Afghanistan

sympathetic to his cause. When Barack Obama became president in 2009, he stated his intent to increase the U.S. military presence in Afghanistan.

THE IRAQ WAR

In 2002, President Bush and other western leaders announced that Iraqi leader Saddam Hussein had "weapons of mass destruction" and connections to al-Qaeda. Weapons of mass destruction include nuclear weapons, chemical weapons, and any other weapon that could kill massive numbers of people. Although Saddam denied having such weapons, U.S. and British intelligence agencies said that he did. Meanwhile, Saddam refused to allow UN investigators into Iraq to confirm his claims. Saddam was supposed to let these

Iraq War

investigators in because it was one of the conditions of his surrender after the Gulf War. The whole world knew that Saddam had used chemical weapons against an ethnic group known as the Kurds in northern Iraq. All these factors led the United States and other nations to conclude that Saddam Hussein was a threat.

In April 2003, the United States led a coalition of nations in an invasion of Iraq. Although it did not have UN support, the invasion quickly succeeded in overthrowing Saddam Hussein. U.S. forces eventually found him hiding in an underground cell. In December 2006, Iraqi authorities hanged Saddam Hussein.

Despite the overthrow of Saddam, however, the **Iraq War** continues. No weapons of mass destruction were ever found. In addition, no one has proven that Saddam actually had ties to al-Qaeda. Meanwhile, the death toll of U.S. soldiers rises as the United States keeps military forces in Iraq to try to prevent the nation from falling into civil war and chaos. Critics of the war say it is time for U.S. troops to come home. Before leaving office, President Bush insisted that U.S. troops must stay until the new Iraqi government is stronger. In January 2009, Barack Obama became president. Obama says that it is time for the Iraqi government to take care of itself. He wants to bring the U.S. forces in Iraq home.

Practice 5.3: Involvement in Southwest Asia

1. Why did the United States become involved in the Gulf War?

2. What happened on September 11, 2001, that increased U.S. involvement in Southwest Asia?

3. What reasons did George W. Bush give for launching the Iraq War?

CHAPTER 5 REVIEW

Key Terms

Southwest Asia
Abraham
Judaism
Jesus
Christianity
Islam
Muhammad
Allah
Qur'an
Ottoman Empire
mandate system
artificial boundaries
anti-Semitism
Holocaust

Zionism
Palestine
Arabs
Palestinians
religious conflict
Cold War
Saddam Hussein
Gulf War
September 11, 2001
al-Qaeda
Osama bin Laden
War on Terror
Afghanistan
Iraq War

Chapter 5 Review Questions

1. The prophet Muhammad founded the religion of

   A. Islam.   B. Christianity.   C. Judaism.   D. Zionism.

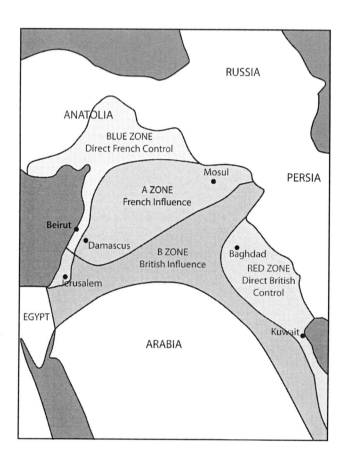

2. What does the map illustrate?

   A. establishment of the modern state of Israel

   B. the Holocaust

   C. mandate system

   D. height of the Ottoman Empire

3. Anti-Semitism is

   A. Jewish nationalism.

   B. one of several religions in Southwest Asia.

   C. racism against Jewish people.

   D. a movement in support of Israel.

4. How did the Holocaust affect Southwest Asia?

   A. The Holocaust put an end to Zionism.

   B. The Holocaust led directly to the spread of Islam.

   C. The Holocaust created support for a Jewish nation in Palestine.

   D. The Holocaust had little effect on Southwest Asia because it happened in Europe.

5. The United States fought the Gulf War because

   A. terrorists attacked the United States.

   B. Iraq invaded Kuwait.

   C. Israel established a modern state in Palestine.

   D. President George W. Bush thought Iraq's leader had weapons of mass destruction.

6. Within three months after September 11, 2001, the United States launched a "War on Terror" by leading an international invasion of

   A. Afghanistan.

   B. Iraq.

   C. the Persian Gulf.

   D. Iran.

Chapter 6
Political and Economic
Understandings of Southwest Asia

This chapter covers the following Georgia standards.

SS7CG4	The student will compare and contrast various forms of government.
SS7CG5	The student will explain the structures of the national governments of Southwest Asia (Middle East).
SS7E5	The student will analyze different economic systems.
SS7E6	The student will explain how voluntary trade benefits buyers and sellers in Southwest Asia (Middle East)
SS7E7	The student will describe factors that influence economic growth and examine their presence or absence in Israel, Saudi Arabia, and Iran.

6.1 GOVERNMENTS OF SOUTHWEST ASIA

Nations of Southwest Asia differ in their forms of government. (Review chapter 3, section 3.1, regarding models of government.)

The Knesset

ISRAEL

Israel's government is a parliamentary democracy. A prime minister (usually the leader of the dominant party in parliament) heads the government. The parliament, called the **Knesset**, serves as the legislative branch of government. Its members are popularly elected by Israeli citizens.

Prime Minister Netanyahu of Israel

SAUDI ARABIA

Saudi Arabia's government is autocratic. It is one of the few **absolute monarchies** in the world today. The king is the head of the government and the unquestioned leader of the country. Saudi Arabia is an Islamic state with the Qur'an and other Muslim teachings providing the basis for its government and laws. The Council of Ministers serves as the king's advisors and helps carry out public policy. It also passes national legislation. But all decrees must be approved by the king.

**King of Saudi Arabia
Abdullah bin Abdul Aziz Al Saud**

IRAN

Iran's government operates as an Islamic republic. It is a theocratic government based on Islam. A theocratic government is often called a **theocracy**. It is a government in which power rests in the hands of religious leaders.

Iran is led by a supreme religious leader. It also has a president. The president serves as the chief executive of the country. But the president's power is limited. Many of his decisions must be approved by the supreme leader.

Iran's Supreme Leader — Ali Khamenei

Iranian citizens elect their president. However, before candidates may run for office, they must be approved by a special council. Iran also has a legislative branch which rules on matters brought before it by the president. Currently, there are eleven women serving in Iran's parliament, more than in any other Southwest Asian nation.

RELIGION AND POLITICS IN SOUTHWEST ASIA

In the United States and many Western nations, religion and politics tend to be separate. In much of Southwest Asia, however, religion and politics are often mixed. Several nations, such as Saudi Arabia and Iran, turn to Islam to define many of the national laws. Even in nations that are more secular, leaders are expected to respect and abide by religious teachings. Israel is a democratic state, but it was

**President of Iran
Mahmoud Ahmadinejad**

founded as a Jewish homeland. Therefore, its politics and culture are very influenced by Judaism. Among predominantly Muslim nations, there are often differences over how much the state should adhere to the Qur'an. Devout Muslims in Saudi Arabia, for instance, are often critical of nations like Turkey and Syria, which are more secular. Religion plays a major role in setting domestic policies, defining the roles of women, writing laws, determining foreign policies, and so forth.

Practice 6.1: Governments of Southwest Asia

1. Which government is an autocratic democracy?

    A. Saudi Arabia

    B. Iran

    C. Israel

    D. United States

2. Which country's government is **least** influenced by Islam?

    A. Saudi Arabia

    B. Israel

    C. Iran

    D. None of the governments above is influenced by Islam.

3. How is the citizen's role in elections more limited in Iran than in Israel?

6.2 Economies of Southwest Asia

Countries have different economic systems. (Review chapter 3, section 3.3 regarding different economic systems.)

Israel's Economy

Thanks largely to aid from the United States, **Israel's economy** is the most developed in Southwest Asia. It is a mixed economy, with both government and private ownership. Lacking in natural resources, Israel depends heavily on imports of petroleum, food products, and military weapons. Israel's high-tech industry is fast developing. It also depends on electronics, biomedical industries, and the production of transport equipment for much of its revenue.

Israeli Currency

SAUDI ARABIA'S ECONOMY

The Saudi government practices a great deal of control over the **Saudi Arabian economy**. The Saudi economy depends predominantly on oil. However, the nation boasts commercial manufacturing and financial industries as well. The government controls all major economic activity. Still, the government is trying to encourage more private business to boost the economy and decrease the nation's dependence on oil. Between five and six million foreign workers also play an important role in the Saudi economy.

Oil Pipeline

TURKEY'S ECONOMY

Turkey's economy is a developed, mixed economy. The country encourages private investment and has a growing private sector. However, the government continues to regulate banks, transportation, communications, and certain other industries.

Turkey's key industries include textiles, oil refineries, iron, steel, food chemicals, and machinery production. In addition to growing industries, Turkey also relies heavily on agriculture. It consistently ranks among the world's top ten nations for agricultural output. Its key agricultural crops include hazelnuts, figs,

Turkish City of Istanbul

pomegranates, watermelons, and cucumbers. Compared to other parts of the economy, however, Turkish agriculture is declining as the nation continues to modernize.

Practice 6.2: Economies of Southwest Asia

1. Which country's economy is controlled by the government and is **most** dependent on oil?

   A. Israel

   B. Turkey

   C. Saudi Arabia

   D. none of the above

2. Describe Turkey's economy.

6.3 OIL AND TRADE

VOLUNTARY TRADE

Like all countries in the world, nations in Southwest Asia depend on trade. A country's location and available natural resources greatly determine what it produces, exports, and imports.

Many nations in Southwest Asia possess large amounts of oil and natural gas. Countries like Saudi Arabia and Kuwait depend on exports of oil and natural gas for much of their wealth. Other nations, such as Israel, Lebanon, and Turkey, which are not as rich in oil, must export other products.

Oil Being Refined for Export

Location is also crucial. Nations along the Mediterranean and in milder areas often have more agricultural products and attract a greater population. Greater population often leads to more industry and higher production. More mountainous regions tend to feature smaller populations and industries like mining. Deserts often provide rich oil supplies, but lack water and other resources to support industries or agriculture.

OIL AND OPEC

Southwest Asia exports a large percentage of the world's **oil**. Nations around the globe depend on oil for energy. Any economic or political instability in Southwest Asia can have worldwide effects. As a result, **OPEC (Organization of Petroleum Exporting Countries)** is very important. OPEC is a group of oil-producing countries, many of which are in the Middle East. These countries work together to look after their economic interests. Together, they decide how much oil will be exported during a given period. Their decisions determine oil

OPEC

prices. The less oil that is made available, the higher the cost of each barrel of oil becomes. OPEC's actions can cause oil shortages in countries like the United States that depend on imports from OPEC nations.

TRADE BARRIERS

As we read in chapter 3, **trade barriers** are an obstacle to trade. They may be natural or political. In Southwest Asia, **natural trade barriers** include deserts and mountainous regions where the terrain makes travel difficult. Since water assists in travel and trade, Southwest Asia's lack of rivers also serves as a natural trade barrier. **Political trade barriers** include embargoes, sanctions, quotas, and tariffs. Examples of political trade barriers include Arab nations' refusals to trade with Israel, the United States imposing sanctions against Iran to protest its nuclear energy program, and the 1973 OPEC oil embargo. (Review chapter 3, section 3.4, regarding trade barriers.)

1973 Oil Embargo in U.S.

FACTORS INFLUENCING ECONOMIC GROWTH

CAPITAL GOODS

Several factors influence a country's **economic growth**. One is its ability to invest in **capital goods**. Capital goods are goods used to produce things. Southwest Asian countries with greater amounts of capital goods tend to be more economically developed.

NATURAL RESOURCES

Another factor is **natural resources**. Oil is a very important natural resource. Any nation rich in oil will export large amounts that produce lots of revenue. Nations rich in other natural resources,

Capital Goods

such as valuable precious metals, will also use them to produce revenue. How valued a nation's natural resources are determines how much revenue they produce and how much foreign investment they attract. For instance, certain nations might allow foreigners to mine, drill, and extract certain resources, in exchange for financial investments that help the country's economy. Foreign investment produces a great deal of wealth for nations like Saudi Arabia.

HUMAN CAPITAL

Human capital refers to investments in the welfare and training of human workers. Providing health care, family benefits, and additional training and education are all examples of investments in human capital. More-developed nations, like Israel, Turkey, and Lebanon, often invest more in human capital than do less-developed nations like Jordan or Afghanistan.

ENTREPRENEURS

For over two thousand years, the Middle East has relied on **entrepreneurs** (people who start and own private businesses). The region features a long tradition of merchants and tradesmen who did business in local markets and/or traveled to foreign lands. Today, some nations in Southwest Asia encourage entrepreneurship, while others place tighter restrictions on what types of businesses may be privately owned.

Southwest Asian Entrepreneur

The more nations are able to invest in capital goods and human capital and the more they encourage entrepreneurship, the more productive their economies tend to be. The usually have a greater GDP than less-developed nations. Valuable natural resources also increase a country's GDP. (Review chapter 3, section 3.4, regarding gross domestic product (GDP).)

Practice 6.3: Oil and Trade

1. What is OPEC? How is it important to Southwest Asia and the rest of the world?

2. What impact does increased investment in capital goods and human capital have on the GDP of nations in Southwest Asia?

CHAPTER 6 REVIEW

Key Terms

Israel's government
Knesset
Saudi Arabia's government
absolute monarchy
Iran's government
theocracy
Israel's economy
Saudi Arabia's economy
Turkey's economy
oil
OPEC (Organization of Petroleum Exporting Countries)

trade barriers
natural trade barriers
political trade barriers
economic growth
capital goods
natural resources
human capital
entrepreneurs

Chapter 6 Review Questions

1. Iran's government is **best** described as a
   A. parliamentary democracy.
   B. presidential democracy.
   C. absolute monarchy.
   D. Islamic republic.

2. What natural resource does Saudi Arabia depend on for **most** of its wealth?
   A. sand
   B. coal
   C. oil
   D. agriculture

3. OPEC is important because it
   A. serves as Israel's parliament.
   B. controls the export of oil from Southwest Asia.
   C. controls how much oil Saudi Arabia and Iran import.
   D. makes sure there are never any oil shortages.

4. In 1973, countries in Southwest Asia refused to export oil to the United States because the U.S. supported Israel in a war. This decision was an example of a
   A. natural trade barrier.
   B. tariff.
   C. embargo.
   D. sanction.

5. Which of the following would be an example of an entrepreneur contributing to economic development?
   A. Mira overcomes discrimination against women in her country and wins a seat in Parliament.
   B. Abdul opens a small shop, eventually builds it into a huge store, and hires thirty employees.
   C. Farouqi leads farmers in a successful movement to win agricultural reforms from their government.
   D. Mohammed gets a job with a foreign business. He works hard and eventually becomes president of the company.

6. Someone who is a member of the Knesset is part of a/an
   A. Islamic republic.
   B. theocracy.
   C. absolute monarchy.
   D. parliamentary democracy.

7. Which of the following is a natural trade barrier in Southwest Asia?
   A. the Persian Gulf
   B. mountains of Afghanistan
   C. Mediterranean Sea
   D. sanctions against Israel

Chapter 7
Geographic Understandings of Southern and Eastern Asia

This chapter covers the following Georgia standards.

SS7G9	The student will locate selected features in Southern and Eastern Asia.
SS7G10	The student will discuss environmental issues across Southern and Eastern Asia.
SS7G11	The student will explain the impact of location, climate, physical characteristics, distribution of natural resources and population distribution on Southern and Eastern Asia.
SS7G12	The student will analyze the diverse cultures of the people who live in Southern and Eastern Asia.

7.1 GEOGRAPHIC FEATURES AND NATIONS OF SOUTHERN AND EASTERN ASIA

GEOGRAPHIC FEATURES

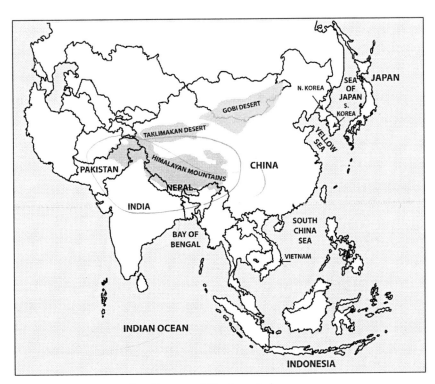

Southern and Eastern Asia

THE HIMALAYAS

The **Himalayan Mountains** in Southern and Eastern Asia are the highest mountains in the world. Mount Everest is more than five miles high and is the tallest mountain on earth. The Himalayas stretch about 1,550 miles across parts of Pakistan, India, Nepal, Bhutan, China, and Myanmar. Lower elevations of the Himalayas can reach summer temperatures as warm as 86°F, while the higher elevations often feature temperatures below freezing.

Himalayas

Various forms of plants and animals live in the Himalayas. Some of these include snow leopards, black bears, marmots, and pandas. Certain people groups inhabit the Himalayas, despite the intense challenges. Perhaps best known are the Sherpa. The Sherpa engage in trade, herd livestock, and raise crops like barley, buckwheat, and potatoes. Famous for their survival skills in the brutal Himalayan environment, they often act as guides for people traveling through the famous mountain chain.

DESERTS

The **Gobi Desert** is a vast stretch of land roughly a thousand miles long and between three hundred and six hundred miles wide. The Gobi Desert lies between the Altai and Hangayn mountains and stretches across parts of Mongolia and China. Much of the Gobi Desert is made up of bare rock rather than sand. Winters are quite harsh. In January the average temperature is –40°F. Spring is typically dry and cold, and the summers are quite warm. In July, there is an average high temperature of about 113°F. Severe dryness limits vegetation. But there are some plants and shrubs that grow. Few people live in the Gobi because of the harsh conditions. Those who do tend to live as nomads. They herd livestock and rely on underground sources of water to survive.

Gobi Desert

The **Taklimakan Desert** is one of the world's largest sandy deserts. It is located in China. The desert is hot in the summer time, but it is cold at night and can drop to temperatures of –4°F. There is very little water in the Taklimakan, making it very hazardous to cross. The only water found is in a few oasis areas.

KOREAN PENINSULA

A **peninsula** is a body of land that extends out into a body of water. It is surrounded on three sides by water. The **Korean Peninsula** is a peninsula bordering China. It is home to the nations of North Korea and South Korea. It stretches about six hundred eighty-four miles long and is very mountainous.

For most of its history, the entire Korean Peninsula was one country united by a common language and culture. After World War II, it was divided into the countries of North and South Korea. The southern portion of the Korean Peninsula usually has a warm and wet climate. The northern portion of the peninsula is usually much colder and has much less rainfall.

MAJOR RIVERS

Many important rivers run throughout Asia. The **Mekong River** is one of the longest rivers in Southern and Eastern Asia. Almost 2,700 miles long, the Mekong runs through western China, Cambodia, Laos, Thailand, and Vietnam before emptying into the South China Sea. It supplies many farmers with the water they need to grow crops. In some areas, people have harnessed the river's power to produce electricity.

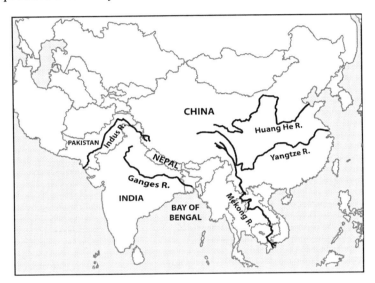

Rivers in South and Eastern Asia

Across northern India and part of Bangladesh runs the **Ganges River**. Beginning in the Himalayas, the Ganges runs about 1,560 miles. It contains many types of fish that people along the river depend on for food. The Ganges also provides water for farming cotton, oilseeds, sugarcane, and other agricultural products. Many Hindus consider the Ganges a sacred river.

Village along the Ganges River

The **Indus River** is the longest river in Pakistan. It is more than 1,900 miles long as it winds through the country before emptying into the Arabian Sea. The Indus serves as Pakistan's key water supply, making it the nation's most important body of water. Pakistanis (people who live in Pakistan) depend on the river to provide water and irrigation for places like Punjab, which sustains much of the country with its agricultural production. Because of the fresh water it provides, a number of Pakistan's key cities lie close to the river or one of its tributaries. A number of industries in the region also depend on the river for survival.

Among China's major rivers are the Huang He and the Yangtze. The **Yangtze River** is China's longest river. It runs almost 3,500 miles across the country. In and near the river are many mineral resources, such as oil, natural gas, copper, and iron ore. The Yangtze is very important to many Chinese farmers. It provides water and nutrients for almost half of China's agriculture. Fishermen rely on the many different types of fish in the Yangtze as well.

The **Huang He River** is China's second-longest river. The Chinese call it the "Yellow River" because of the color of the silt that covers the ground along its shores. The Huang He often overflows, causing deadly and destructive flooding. For this reason, the Chinese also call it "China's sorrow." The Huang He begins in Tibet and runs east to the Yellow Sea.

OCEANS AND SEAS

The **Indian Ocean** makes up nearly one-fifth of all the ocean water in the world. It stretches more than 6,200 miles from the southern tip of Africa to Australia. The Indian Ocean reaches to Asia in the north and Antarctica in the south. For centuries, traders, naval fleets, and other travelers have relied on the Indian Ocean to connect Asia to Europe and Africa.

Boat in the Indian Ocean

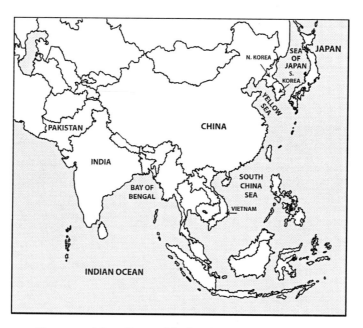

Oceans and Seas Located in Southern and Eastern Asia

The **Bay of Bengal** lies to the northeast of the Indian Ocean. It provides many different types of fish for people in the region. The Bay also provides ports for shipping and has historically been an important body of water for international trade.

The **Yellow Sea** lies between China and the Korean Peninsula. Its name comes from the color of the silt-laden water that runs into it from some of China's major rivers. The Yellow Sea serves as an important water trade route and is home to a number of important sea ports.

The coasts of Japan, Russia, and Korea all line the **Sea of Japan**. From December to March, winds carry cold and dry polar air over the warm waters of the sea. This causes snow to fall on the west coast of Japan. In the summer, tropical winds cause dense fog. The winter winds bring rough seas which crash onto the Japanese coasts.

The **South China Sea** provides seafood for many people in East Asia. Many ships travel across the South China Sea, carrying food, oil, and other goods. Throughout the year, monsoons (strong storms involving high winds and heavy rain) blow across the sea, greatly affecting agriculture. Like other major bodies of water, the South China Sea has always played a crucial role in travel and trade.

NATIONS OF SOUTHERN AND EASTERN ASIA

INDIA

The Republic of **India** is located in southern Asia and borders the Arabian Sea, the Bay of Bengal, Burma, and Pakistan. The capital of India is New Delhi. The national language is Hindi, but thousands of Indians speak local languages too. English is officially used for government and business. India has the second-largest population in the world with nearly 1.12 billion citizens. The two main religions of India are Hinduism and Islam.

Indian Culture

India consists of three main regions: peninsular India, the Indo-Gangetic Plain, and the Himalayas. Peninsular India is the portion of India that juts out into the Arabian Sea and the Indian Ocean. The upper half of the peninsula contains many mountain ranges and plateaus. The few people who live in this area are herders or grain farmers. The bottom half of the peninsula contains the Eastern and Western Ghats mountain chains and the Deccan Plateau. The Gangetic Plain region is north of peninsular India and consists of lowlands that produce most of India's agriculture.

India's Taj Mahal

The Gangetic Plain includes many river systems, such as the Indus River and the Ganges River. These rivers help to water the many crops grown in the region. The Himalayan mountain region lies along the northern and eastern borders of India. Some of the highest peaks in the world are in this region.

CHINA

The **People's Republic of China** is a country in eastern Asia. China has the world's largest population: over 1.3 billion people. The major ethnic groups are Han Chinese, Zhuang, Manchu, Hui, and Miao. The main language is Mandarin, but other dialects, such as Cantonese, are spoken as well. China is officially an atheist country (does not sanction religion), but many people practice Daoism (Taoism), Buddhism, Islam, and Christianity. The capital of China is Beijing.

Chinese Culture

China can be divided into three geographic regions. One of these regions is the Plateau of Tibet. It stands an average of about thirteen thousand feet above sea level. This is the highest highland area in the world. It is often called the "rooftop of the world."

Tibetan Monks

VIETNAM

Vietnam is located in Southeastern Asia and borders the Gulf of Thailand, Gulf of Tonkin, the South China Sea, Laos, and Cambodia. It is home to about 85.2 million people. Although most are Vietnamese, many Chinese and members of other ethnic groups live there as well. Buddhism, Hoa Hao, Cao Dai, and Christianity are the main religions.

Vietnamese Culture

Summers in northern Vietnam are extremely hot with heavy rainfall. Southern Vietnam has an average annual temperature of 74°F. In central and southern Vietnam, between June and November, monsoon winds usher in rains and typhoons (hurricanes). These rains and typhoons generally hit the mountain and lowland plains regions. Between December and April, the climate is typically dry and windy because of the northeast monsoon. The southernmost portion of Vietnam experiences high temperatures during this period.

INDONESIA

The nation of **Indonesia** lies between the Indian and Pacific oceans and is made up of thousands of islands in Southeastern Asia. The capital of Indonesia is Jakarta. Nearly 245.5 million people live in Indonesia. The major ethnic groups are Javanese, Sundanese, Madurese, and coastal Malays. Indonesian is the official language. Islam is the major religion.

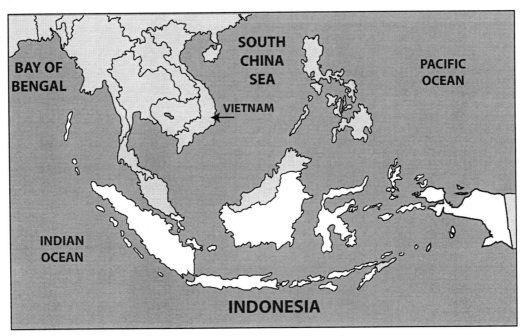

Indonesian Islands

Temperatures in Indonesia are typically high throughout the year. Average temperatures range from 74°F to 88°F. The Maoke Mountains of Papua is the only area high enough for snow to fall. Across most of Indonesia, it rains heavily throughout the year. The greatest rainfall occurs between December and March. During the dry season, from June to October, there is little rain in certain areas of the country.

Most of the major islands of Indonesia are made up of volcanic mountains and are covered with tropical forests. The islands also contain coastal plains covered by swamps. The coasts are bordered by shallow seas and coral reefs.

There are many different people groups in Indonesia. One group, the Papuans, maintain little contact with the rest of the world. They live a primitive lifestyle, based on ancient customs. Groups similar to the Papuans are found throughout remote parts of Indonesia.

Indonesians

NORTH AND SOUTH KOREA

North Korea occupies the northern half of the Korean Peninsula. It borders China and South Korea. The Yellow Sea lies to its west and the Sea of Japan lies to its east. The capital of North Korea is Pyongyang.

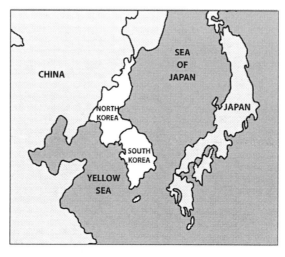

Korean Peninsula

North Korea has a population of 23.1 million people. Korean is the official language. It is a communist nation that does not support religion. But religion is still practiced by many North Koreans. The main religions are Buddhism, Confucianism, Shamanism, Cheondoism, and Christianity.

North Korean Leader Kim Jong IL

South Korea covers the southern half of the Korean Peninsula. The capital of South Korea is Seoul. Nearly forty-nine million people live in South Korea. The main religions which are practiced in South Korea are Christianity, Buddhism, Shamanism, Confucianism, and Cheondoism.

Seoul, South Korea

JAPAN

Japan is made up of islands. It lies between the North Pacific Ocean and the Sea of Japan. The capital of Japan is Tokyo. There are nearly 128 million people in Japan. Japanese is the national language, and nearly everyone who lives in Japan is ethnically Japanese. The two major religions are Shinto and Buddhism.

Japanese Culture

While much of southern and eastern Asia is relatively poor, Japan is the second-richest country in the world. Japan's wealth and success can be attributed to many things. Some of these include a well-educated and dedicated work force, efficient experts and leaders, and high savings and investment rates. While Japan has few natural resources, it can purchase what it needs using money made from its many industries. Japan is one of the world's largest producers of motor vehicles, steel, and high-tech goods.

Practice 7.1: Geographic Features and Nations of Southeast Asia

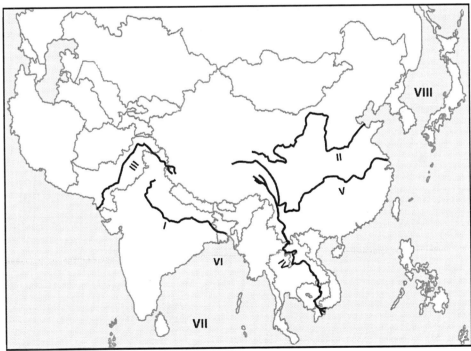

1. Look at the map above. What body of water does the Roman numeral IV represent?

   A. Bay of Bengal

   B. Sea of Japan

   C. Indus River

   D. Mekong River

2. Look on the previous page at the same map used to answer question #1. Which body of water borders both Japan and the Korean Peninsula?
   A. V C. VII
   B. VI D. VIII

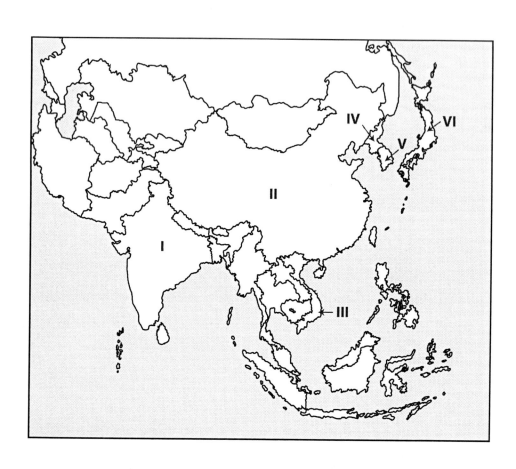

3. Look at the map above. Which countries border one another?
   A. Japan and North Korea C. China and North Korea
   B. Japan and South Korea D. Vietnam and North Korea

4. Which country on the map has the world's largest population?
   A. I C. III
   B. II D. VI

5. In which country would one find the Indus River?
   A. I C. V
   B. III D. VI

7.2 ENVIRONMENTAL ISSUES

WATER POLLUTION

Like all countries, nations in Southern and Eastern Asia face environmental issues. Pollution, maintaining wildlife, and protecting the natural environment are all examples of environmental issues.

Water pollution is a problem in Southern and Eastern Asia. As the population grows, more and more people depend on water from rivers like the Ganges and the Yangtze. People who live in rural villages along these rivers often use them as sewers and places to dump their trash. In more developed areas, waste from factories can pollute the rivers. Since people use these bodies of water to bathe, gather drinking water, and wash clothes, pollution can cause serious health problems and lead to the spread of disease.

India's Water Pollution

AIR POLLUTION

Air pollution is also a problem in Southern and Eastern Asia. Many large cities exist in the region. Often, these cities have many industries. These industries help the economy, but they can also lead to more pollution from factories. The large populations in these cities also increase pollution. The greater the population, the more people use resources, discard trash, dispose of waste, and so on. China and India must especially deal with the effects of pollution because of their huge populations. They have many overcrowded cities. Their factories often lack many of the modern technologies that help industries in more developed nations to combat pollution.

Air Pollution in China

FLOODING

Much of Southern and Eastern Asia experiences wet and dry seasons. During the wet seasons, heavy rainfalls occur regularly. These heavy rains often cause rivers to overflow and cause floods. **Flooding** occurs when water rises and covers areas that are normally dry. When rivers in Asia flood, it can be deadly. Many people in flooded areas are killed or left homeless. Floods can also cause **mudslides**. When flooding or

Asian Flooding

heavy rains occur, the ground can turn to mud. Sometimes this mud will break loose and slide down the side of mountains, destroying buildings and covering entire villages. Even if people survive the floods and mudslides, the damage done to crops can often result in mass starvation.

Practice 7.2: Environmental Issues

1. Describe how the pollution of rivers can lead to health problems and disease.

2. How does flooding impact people in Southern and Eastern Asia?

7.3 CLIMATE, LOCATION, AND PEOPLES OF SOUTHERN AND EASTERN ASIA

IMPACT OF CLIMATE

The climate of Southern and Eastern Asia has been a major factor in determining what agricultural products and industries have development in the region. The humid and tropical climate that covers most of the region has helped to develop a large variety of plant life and vegetation. One of the most important crops in the region is rice. Other important crops include corn, cassava, and legumes.

Hot vs. Cold Climates

Some countries, like Japan, have fewer natural resources. For this reason, Japan has focused on developing its manufacturing industries. Those countries where crops have been plentiful are able to rely more on their agricultural industries. Meanwhile, areas of the region that present more challenging climates, such as the Himalayas or the Gobi Desert, have produced little in the way of new industries or economic development.

GEOGRAPHY'S IMPACT ON PEOPLE

As we have learned from our readings, geographic location affects where people live. It also impacts the work they do and how they travel from place to place. In the Himalayas, people are more isolated and often depend on subsistence farming and herding for survival. In the Gobi Desert, nomadic herding is the normal way of life. In fertile rural areas, much of the population lives as poor farmers or small village artisans or merchants. In urban areas, people often work in factories and live in overcrowded, polluted areas. In cities and surrounding areas, cars, buses, and

Urban Citizens in Beijing

trains are common forms of transportation. In especially crowded cities, like Beijing, people often ride bikes because the immense population makes it impossible for everyone to drive cars. Rural areas still rely heavily on rivers and streams to travel by water.

Herders in the Himalayas

Rural Chinese Farmers

RELIGIONS OF SOUTHERN AND EASTERN ASIA

HINDUISM

Prambanan Hindu Temple in Indonesia

Hinduism is one of the oldest and largest religions in the world. It dates back to roughly 1500 BC (earlier than Buddhism, Judaism, Christianity, and Islam). The word *hindu* means "the people who live near the Indus River." The religion gets its name because it originated thousands of years ago among people of the Indus River Valley who had migrated from central Asia.

Hinduism is polytheistic (believes in many gods). Traditionally, Hindus believe in a caste system. A "caste" is a particular class into which a person is born. Some groups are more respected and superior to others. The Hindu caste system of India has five groups. *Brahmans* are the priests and the most respected caste. Next come the *Kshatriyas*. They are the nobles and warriors. The *Vaishyas* are merchants and farmers. *Shudras* are those who serve the Brahmans, Kshatriyas, and Vaishyas. Finally, *Untouchables* form the bottom caste. They are not even allowed to touch or live near members of the upper castes.

Hindus also believe in reincarnation and karma. Reincarnation is the belief that, after someone dies, they are reborn as a new person. Under strict Hinduism, a person can switch castes only through reincarnation. Karma is the spiritual consequence of what someone does. Good deeds produce "good karma," and bad deeds produce "bad karma." If one's good karma outweighs their bad karma, then they will likely be reincarnated into a higher caste. However, if one's bad karma is greater, then they may be reincarnated into a lower caste, or even as an animal. Hindus hope to collect enough good karma to achieve moksha (salvation). Moksha requires several lifetimes and allows the soul to break the cycle of rebirth by uniting with the "World Soul," known as *Brahma*. Although Hinduism spread to a few other parts of Asia, it predominantly stayed in India until after 100 AD.

Ganesh, a Hindu God

BUDDHISM

Buddha

Buddhism also started in India. Unlike Hinduism, Buddhism does not center around the worship of any gods. Instead, it centers around meditation and a quest for inner enlightenment (understanding of truth). Buddhism began around 500 BC when a prince named Siddhartha Gautama began a spiritual search to understand suffering and how to overcome it. He advocated the "Middle Way" as the path to a state of eternal enlightenment called nirvana. The Middle Way rejected both the indulgences of the world and the extreme self-denial of other religious teachers. After a long period of meditation, Siddhartha proclaimed that he had received the enlightenment he sought. He became known to his followers as the "Buddha" (enlightened one) and began spreading his teachings to other parts of India. Many Indians liked Buddhism because it rejected the caste system. Following Buddha's death in 483 BC, his followers spread Buddhism to other parts of Asia. In 300 BC, India's King Ashoka became a Buddhist and helped spread Buddhism as well. Following ancient trade routes, Buddhism reached China, Japan, and other parts of East Asia. Buddhist missionaries also carried the faith west to parts of Europe and Africa. By the end of the tenth century, most Buddhists lived in regions of Asia outside India.

ISLAM

Islam is also a major religion in southern and eastern Asia. Indonesia has the largest Muslim population in the world. India also has a large number of Muslims. Following India's independence in 1947, Muslims founded the independent Islamic state of Pakistan in what had been the northwest portion of the country. (Review chapter 4, section 4.3, and chapter 5, section 5.1, regarding the history and beliefs of Islam.)

Islam in Indonesia

SHINTO

Shinto is a major religion in Japan. Many followers of Shinto believe in many gods. They also believe that all natural things, not just people and animals, have souls and spirits. Shinto involves many religious rituals. Most people in Japan practice some form of Shinto. Shinto is also practiced in other countries outside East Asia. It is no longer only a Japanese religion.

Shinto

CONFUCIANISM

Confucianism is a philosophical system originating in China around 500 BC. Its founder is the Chinese philosopher Confucius. It does not focus on the worship of any god. Instead, it teaches a system of moral behavior. It stresses the importance of education as a key path to molding moral people. It teaches that societies should strive to be led by the moral virtue within people rather than by the forceful hand of any government. Confucianism is very popular in China, Korea, Vietnam, and other parts of southern and eastern Asia.

CHRISTIANITY

Christianity is also practiced in Southern and Eastern Asia. One of the largest Christian Churches in the world is located in Seoul, South Korea. In recent years, the number of professing Christians has grown in countries like China as well.

LITERACY

As we have learned from earlier chapters, **literacy** (the ability to read and write) is very important for a nation's development. Like most other parts of the world, Southern and Eastern Asian nations work to try and improve their countries' literacy rates. More-developed nations, like Japan and South Korea, have high literacy rates. Less-developed nations, like India, tend to have lower literacy rates. High literacy means that a population is educated and prepared to compete with the rest of the world politically and economically. The more nations increase their literacy rate, the easier time they have growing economically and improving their citizens' quality of life.

Education in Japan

Practice 7.3: Climate, Location, and People of Southern and Eastern Asia

1. Describe how geography can impact what people in Southern and Eastern Asia do for a living.

2. The oldest major religion in the world is
   A. Shinto.   B. Islam.   C. Hinduism.   D. Buddhism.

3. **Most** people in Japan practice some form of
   A. Islam.   C. Confucianism.
   B. Hinduism.   D. Shinto.

4. Confucianism is **best** described as
   A. a religion that worships many gods.
   B. the most important religion in Japan.
   C. a philosophical system that emphasizes moral teachings.
   D. a philosophy founded by an South Asian prince.

CHAPTER 7 REVIEW

Key Terms

Himalayan Mountains
Gobi Desert
Taklimakan Desert
peninsula
Korean Peninsula
Mekong River
Ganges River
Indus River
Yangtze River
Huang He River
Indian Ocean
Bay of Bengal
Yellow Sea
Sea of Japan
South China Sea
India

People's Republic of China
Vietnam
Indonesia
North Korea
South Korea
Japan
water pollution
air pollution
flooding
mudslides
Hinduism
Buddhism
Islam
Shinto
Confucianism
literacy

Chapter 7 Review Questions

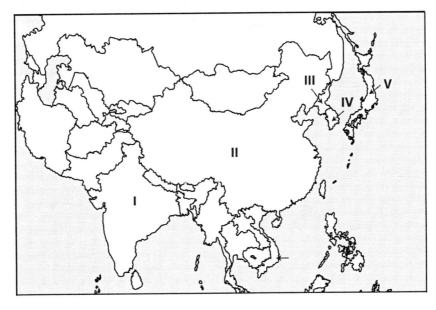

1. Which of the following areas on the map is the **most** developed economically?

   A. I   B. V   C. III   D. II

2. In which area on the map above would one find the **highest** population of Hindus?

   A. I   B. II   C. IV   D. V

3. In which area on the map above did Confucianism begin?

   A. I   B. II   C. III   D. IV

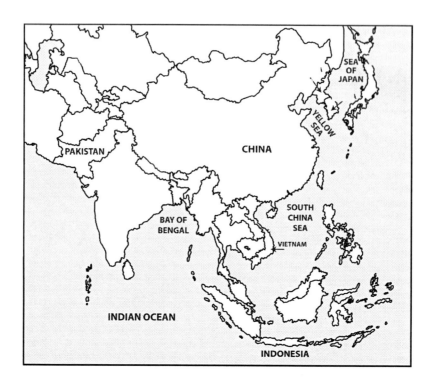

4. Someone traveling from Indonesia to Vietnam would cross the
   A. Bay of Bengal.   C. Sea of Japan.

   B. South China Sea.   D. Yellow Sea.

5. Which body of water touches India?
   A. Yellow Sea   C. Bay of Bengal

   B. South China Sea   D. Sea of Japan

6. Someone traveling from Korea to Japan would cross the
   A. Yellow Sea.   C. Bay of Bengal.

   B. Sea of Japan.   D. Indian Ocean.

7. Most people in Japan practice some form of
   A. Buddhism.   B. Islam.   C. Confucianism.   D. Shinto.

8. Villages along the Yangtze and Ganges rivers often have to worry about the threat of
   A. civil war.   C. flooding.

   B. desertification.   D. all of the above

9. Most people in India practice
   A. Islam.   B. Hinduism.   C. Shinto.   D. Buddhism.

10. Which of the following is a nation made up of islands?
    A. Japan   B. China   C. Vietnam   D. North Korea

Chapter 8
Historical Understandings of Southern and Eastern Asia

This chapter covers the following Georgia standard.

SS7H3	The student will analyze continuity and change in Southern and Eastern Asia leading to the 21st century.

8.1 JAPAN, CHINA, AND INDIA

Japan began to modernize during the nineteenth century. It opened several ports to trade with the United States and European powers. Japan built railroads and factories. It also modernized its military with updated weapons and built a modern navy modeled after those in Europe. Eventually, Japan replaced China as the most powerful nation in Eastern Asia.

Map of Japan

POST-WWII JAPAN

During the first half of the twentieth century, Japan decided to use force to expand its territory. It invaded China in 1937 and soon gained control of many of China's coastal cities. It failed, however, to capture China's interior. From there, the Japanese invaded other parts of Asia as well.

Eventually, Japan pulled the United States into the war when it launched a surprise attack on the U.S. naval fleet anchored at Pearl Harbor, Hawaii. Japan used the element of surprise and a well-trained military to win early battles in the war. Over time, however, the United States and its allies proved too powerful. They defeated Japan in 1945.

Emperor Hirohito of Japan

THE U.S. ROLE IN REBUILDING JAPAN

Following the war, the United States oversaw the rebuilding of Japan. It helped draft a new constitution. The new constitution established a democratic government, reduced the size of Japan's military, and modified the role of the emperor. It also guaranteed certain human rights and extended women the right to vote.

In 1951, Japan became independent again. However, it kept a close relationship with the United States. The United States poured large amounts of money into rebuilding Japan and helped it grow economically. Today, Japan is one of the wealthiest and economically strongest nations in the world.

General Douglas MacArthur and Emperor Hirohito

CONCERNS ABOUT COMMUNISM

One reason the United States wanted to strengthen Japan's economy was due to concerns about **communism**. In a communist state, people have very little freedom and the state owns almost all the property. People in poorer nations are often attracted to communism. They think it will produce more economic equality. The United States did not want communism to spread. It saw communism as a threat to freedom and democracy. The U.S. government felt that it needed to help nations like Japan rebuild and grow economically so that the people would not be drawn to communism.

CHINA

During the late nineteenth century and into the twentieth, **China** grew very unstable. Poverty and starvation led to unrest among many of China's peasants. In 1912, a revolution replaced the emperor with a Chinese republic. But the republic proved too weak to maintain control. Local warlords began to raise their own armies and seize control of different parts of the country. Many of these warlords went to war with one another. Out of this unrest, two major parties arose: the Nationalist Party, under the leadership of Chiang Kai-shek; and the **Communist Party**, under the leadership of **Mao Zedong**.

Mao Zedong in the 1940s

Tensions soon mounted between the Nationalists and Communists. The Nationalists favored capitalism. They wanted to allow private ownership of businesses, factories, and property. The Communists wanted a command economy with land, property, and businesses in the hands of the state. The Communists argued that only such an economy would ease the suffering of China's poor rural population.

China's Communist Revolution

In 1927, Chiang Kai-shek attacked the Communists, almost destroying them. Mao and many of his followers, however, escaped. In 1937, Japan's invasion of China temporarily put an end to the China's civil war. Both the Nationalists and the Communists turned their attention to fighting the Japanese. After World War II, however, the civil war resumed.

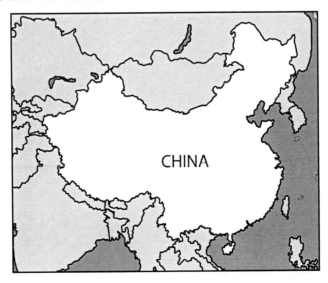

China

MAO'S RISE TO POWER

Following World War II, the United States backed China's Nationalist Party. The Soviet Union backed the Communists. Millions of China's peasants and farmers flocked to Mao's cause. By 1949, Mao's Communists had won control of the country, forcing Chiang and his Nationalists to flee to the island of Formosa, known today as Taiwan.

THE GREAT LEAP FORWARD

Once in power, Mao sought to modernize China. He wanted to build industries and strengthen the country. In 1958, he launched the **Great Leap Forward**. The Great Leap Forward was based on the communist ideal of every citizen working together for the good of the community and the state. It involved thousands of Chinese citizens living together in communes. They shared land for farming, worked together in factories, and tried to care for needs.

Great Leap Forward

Unfortunately, the Great Leap Forward was a huge failure. Floods, droughts, bad management, and corruption ruined China and left millions dying of starvation. Eventually, the people returned to their small villages and towns to work on government-owned land or in state-owned factories.

THE CULTURAL REVOLUTION

Following the Great Leap Forward, opposition to Mao grew within the Communist Party. In order to maintain power, Mao launched the **Cultural Revolution** in 1966. Relying heavily on a youth militia known as the Red Guard, Mao removed his political enemies and seized tighter control of the government. Mao's regime executed over half a million people as enemies of the state. Many of them were writers, professors, politicians, artists, and religious leaders whose influence Mao viewed as a threat. Mao declared the Cultural Revolution over in 1969. In reality, his harsh persecution of his critics continued until his death in 1976.

Cultural Revolution

TIANANMEN SQUARE

Mao died in 1976. But China's Communist Party continued to rule with an iron fist. They often violated human rights. The government imprisoned and executed many people who disagreed with the government.

In 1989, an incident occurred at **Tiananmen Square** that focused international attention on China. A series of protests broke out between April 15 and June 3. Many of the protesters demanded democracy in China. Others protested the country's inflation and rising unemployment rate. By June, there were hundreds of thousands of protestors.

Student Blocking Tanks – Tiananmen Square

On the evening of June 3, army tanks rolled into Tiananmen Square to crush the protests. Chinese officials killed hundreds of people and wounded thousands more. The government also arrested and executed many of those who participated. The international community was shocked, and a number of countries (including the United States) publicly condemned the action. Someone with a video camera filmed the most lasting image of Tiananmen Square. It showed one lone protester as he blocked the path of four single-file tanks. To this day, no one is sure whom that protester was, or what became of him.

INDIA

Following World War II, European colonization began to crumble. **India's independence movement** that began prior to the war gained strength. For decades, Indians lived under the rule of the British Empire. They suffered discrimination and unjust treatment in their own country. **Mohandas Gandhi** was a Hindu who believed in nonviolent protest as a means of gaining freedom from Great Britain. Gandhi led a successful independence movement, in which he and his followers willingly endured beatings, imprisonment, and even death at the hands of British authorities. All the while, they peacefully refused to obey unjust laws. Their passive resistance won the support of outsiders and even many British citizens. It caused Indian nationalism (national pride and a desire for independence on the part of Indians) to grow. Gandhi's efforts led to India's independence in 1947.

Mohandas Gandhi

Practice 8.1: Japan, China, and India

1. Which of the following nations did the United States play a major role in rebuilding after World War II?

   A. Japan   B. China   C. India   D. Tiananmen

2. Which nation became a communist state after World War II?

   A. Japan   B. China   C. India   D. Tiananmen

3. Which nation won independence largely through nonviolent resistance?
   A. Japan   B. China   C. India   D. Tiananmen

4. Describe the Great Leap Forward.

5. Describe the Cultural Revolution. Why did Mao launch it?

8.2 KOREA AND VIETNAM

The Korean Peninsula

THE KOREAN WAR

The Allies liberated **Korea** from the Japanese during World War II. Since both the Soviet Union and the United States played a role in its liberation, the country was divided along the 38th parallel (line of latitude running through Korea). **North Korea** allied with the Soviet Union as a communist state. **South Korea** became a pro-U.S., capitalist society.

In 1950, the **Korean War** began when North Korean troops crossed the 38th parallel and invaded South Korea. The United Nations sent troops to help South Korea. General Douglas

Korean War

MacArthur (the same man who had overseen Japan after the war) commanded the UN troops. MacArthur's forces successfully pushed the North Koreans all the way back to the northernmost parts of Korea. Things changed again, however, when Chinese troops crossed the border to help North Korea. A stalemate soon developed, in which neither side could gain an advantage. Both sides signed a cease-fire in 1953 that left the country divided at almost the exact same point as it had been before the war.

Today, tensions remain high between North and South Korea. Capitalism and democracy have allowed South Korea to thrive as a wealthy, modernized society. Meanwhile, North Korea is one of the poorest nations in the world. Its strict communist regime pours most of the nation's resources into its military rather than on efforts to modernize and benefit the population.

VIETNAM

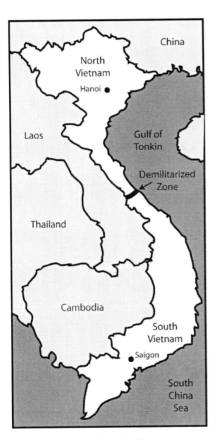

North and South Vietnam

Ho Chi Minh

After Japan's defeat, France tried to reassert its control over Indo-China (Vietnam, Cambodia, and Laos). In **Vietnam**, a nationalist movement under the leadership of **Ho Chi Minh** rose up to resist the French. Ho Chi Minh's success concerned the United States because they viewed him as a communist. In 1954, the Vietnamese and Western powers reached a compromise. They divided Vietnam into two nations. North Vietnam fell under the communist rule of Ho Chi Minh, while a U.S.-backed government ruled South Vietnam.

THE VIETNAM WAR

Before long, war broke out between North and South Vietnam. The United States sent military advisors and eventually troops to help the South Vietnamese resist communist forces. The United States feared that communism would spread throughout all of Eastern Asia if South Vietnam fell. Upon arrival, the U.S. found itself fighting not only North Vietnam's invading army, but also South Vietnamese communists, known as the Vietcong. The Vietcong consisted largely of poor rural farmers who felt they would fare much better under communism. Many Vietnamese citizens also backed Ho Chi Minh because they saw him as a nationalist leader. They

Vietnam War

resented the years of French colonization and did not want the United States or European powers having influence over their country.

Although not nearly as modern or well-supplied as the U.S. forces, the Vietcong and North Vietnamese launched an effective *guerilla war*. In guerilla warfare, a weaker enemy attacks quickly and unexpectedly, then slips away before its enemy can fully retaliate. It hopes to inflict enough damage that its stronger enemy will lose its will to fight. As years passed and more and more U.S. soldiers died in Vietnam, guerilla warfare eventually succeeded. In 1973, the United States formally ended its military involvement in Vietnam.

Soon after the U.S. troops left, the communists began their fight again. In April 1975, the South Vietnamese capital of Saigon fell. After decades of struggle, the communists finally had all of Vietnam in their grasp.

Practice 8.2: Korea and Vietnam

1. Why did the United States become involved in Korea and Vietnam?

2. What were the results of the Korean and Vietnam Wars?

CHAPTER 8 REVIEW

Key Terms

Japan
communism
China
China's Communist Party
Mao Zedong
Great Leap Forward
Cultural Revolution
Tiananmen Square

India's independence movement
Mohandas Gandhi
Korea
North Korea
South Korea
Korean War
Vietnam
Ho Chi Minh

Chapter 8 Review Questions

1. The photo above **most likely** depicts

   A. the Cultural Revolution.

   B. Tiananmen Square.

   C. the Korean War.

   D. India's independence movement.

2. The Great Leap Forward was meant to promote

   A. the communist ideal of everyone working together for the community and the state.

   B. India's independence movement through nonviolent protest.

   C. Mao's power by removing all of his political enemies and educating the Chinese youth.

   D. Japan's economy after WWII so that the nation would not fall to communism.

3. Mohandas Gandhi was a nationalist leader in
   A. India.
   C. China.
   B. Japan.
   D. Vietnam.

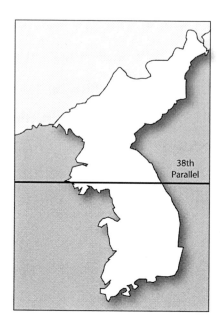

4. The map above depicts
   A. Vietnam.   B. China.   C. India.   D. Korea.

5. Today, which of the following nations is a capitalist democracy?
   A. North Korea   B. China   C. Japan   D. Vietnam

6. The photo above was **most likely** taken during the
   A. rebuilding of Japan.
   C. Great Leap Forward.
   B. Cultural Revolution.
   D. Gandhi's independence movement.

Chapter 9
Political & Economic Understandings
of Southern and Eastern Asia

This chapter covers the following Georgia standards.

SS7CG6	The student will compare and contrast various forms of government.
SS7CG7	The student will demonstrate an understanding of national governments in Southern and Eastern Asia.
SS7E8	The student will analyze different economic systems.
SS7E9	The student will explain how voluntary trade benefits buyers and sellers in Southern and Eastern Asia.
SS7E10	The student will describe factors that influence economic growth and examine their presence or absence in India, China, and Japan.

9.1 GOVERNMENTS AND ECONOMIES OF SOUTHERN AND EASTERN ASIA

GOVERNMENTS OF SOUTHERN AND EASTERN ASIA

INDIA'S GOVERNMENT

India's government operates as a federal republic and a parliamentary democracy. (Review chapter 3, section 3.1, regarding a parliamentary democracy.) Citizens elect officials to make decisions on their behalf. Power is divided between the national and state governments. Unlike in the United States, the national government still has ultimate authority over all state matters.

India's Government

The central government has three branches: executive, legislative, and judicial. The executive branch consists of the president, vice president, prime minister, and Council of Ministers. The president serves as the chief of state and acts as the nation's chief representative. He or she appoints state governors, members of the Council of Ministers, and the prime minister. Most of the president's duties are only ceremonial, however, because these offices have already been won in elections.

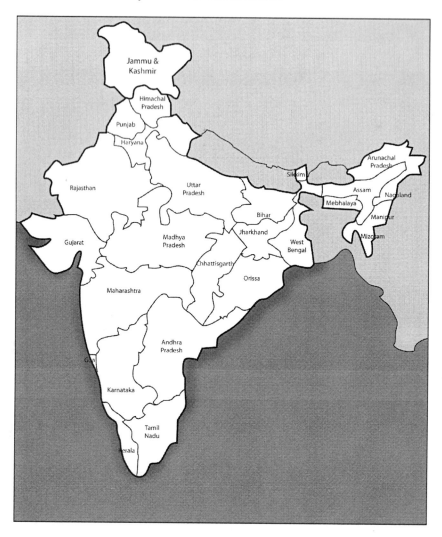

India's Twenty-eight States

Most of the real power rests with the prime minister and the Council of Ministers. The prime minister is the leader of the government and India's top official. The leader of the majority party in parliament serves as the prime minister. The Council of Ministers serves as the prime minister's body of advisors. It helps lead various government departments.

India's parliament serves as the legislative branch. It passes the country's laws. The judicial branch consists of India's supreme court.

CHINA'S GOVERNMENT

China's government operates under a **one-party system** (only one political party has any power). All the country's political power rests with **China's Communist Party**. China is an authoritative state with citizens holding limited power. Even when there are elections, citizens can only choose from candidates pre-approved by the party.

Hu Jintao, General Secretary China's Communist Party

China's government consists of three branches: executive, legislative, and judicial. However, since all three are under the firm control of the party, there is no real separation of powers. China's executive branch of government includes the president, vice president, premier, vice premier, and State Council. The Chinese president is the chief of state and speaks for China to the international community. The premier is like a prime minister and actually runs the government.

The National People's Congress (NPC) serves as China's legislature. It chooses both the president and vice president. It is a unicameral body (only one house). Its main role is to review laws sent to it by the executive branch. Again, since all the leaders are part of the Communist Party, the NPC almost always passes the laws.

Chinese Soldiers

China's Supreme People's Court makes up the judicial branch. Unlike many other countries, this branch is not independent from the executive branch. It has no power to challenge actions of the other two branches. Its role is to make sure the people obey communist laws.

JAPAN'S GOVERNMENT

Japan's government is a **constitutional monarchy**. It has an emperor, but he cannot do whatever he wants. He is restricted by the nation's constitution. The emperor acts as the head of state but has very little power. The real power rests with the prime minister and the **Diet** (Japan's legislative body). Japan operates as a parliamentary democracy.

Japan's Prime Minister Hatoyama

The government has three branches: executive, legislative, and judicial. The executive branch includes the emperor, a prime minister, and the cabinet. The prime minister leads the government and appoints the cabinet. The cabinet helps the prime minister lead the country.

The legislative branch consists of a bicameral body called the Diet. It consists of two houses. Japanese citizens elect the members of the Diet, who are responsible for making the laws of the country. Japan's supreme court heads its judicial branch. It has complete independence and makes sure the other branches carry out their duties according to the constitution.

Japan's Diet in Session

ECONOMIES OF SOUTHERN AND EASTERN ASIA

INDIA'S ECONOMY

India's economy is a mixed economy. The government still controls industries and businesses to some degree, but not nearly as much as it once did. After years of operating as a command economy, India has changed course in the last couple of decades. Leaders discovered that state-controlled production hurt India's economy. In the last twenty years, India has allowed more private ownership and market competition. As a result, India's economy has grown tremendously, and the country is becoming a major player in world trade and international business.

Indian Currency

CHINA'S ECONOMY

China's economy is a mixed economy that leans toward a command system. However, in the last twenty years, China has modernized its economy and adopted certain characteristics of a market economy. The government allows some private industry and even foreign-owned businesses. The number of state-owned factories has dropped sharply. Most businesses are now expected to make a profit and pay the salaries of their own employees. China

Chinese Industry

continues to move in the direction of a market economy in order to make production more efficient and meet the needs of its massive population. Still, the government exercises stricter control than in nations like Japan or the United States.

Rural Chinese Farmers

JAPAN'S ECONOMY

Japan's economy is a thriving market economy. Japan is one of the wealthiest nations in the world. Prices of goods and services are based on supply and demand (what consumers want and what producers are willing to produce). The government owns very little industry, and trade remains mostly unrestricted.

Japanese Products

Tokyo's Economy

NORTH KOREA'S ECONOMY

North Korea's economy is one of the poorest in the world. The strict communist government controls the nation's economy. Production is inefficient and creates very little wealth for the nation. What little money the nation does have goes to the military rather than to help the country's starving population. Most North Koreans live in extreme poverty. They have very little say in their government and few means to improve their income or way of life.

Poverty in North Korea

SOUTH KOREA'S ECONOMY

South Korea's economy is a mixed economy that favors free markets. Capitalism has made South Korea a relatively wealthy nation with a much higher standard of living than North Korea. It trades with many nations.

Practice 9.1: Governments and Economies of Southern and Eastern Asia

1. Which of the following countries is a constitutional monarchy?
   A. North Korea   B. South Korea   C. Japan   D. India

2. Which of the following nations is a communist state?
   A. India   B. China   C. Japan   D. South Korea

3. Which of the following nations has the poorest economy?
   A. North Korea   B. Japan   C. South Korea   D. China

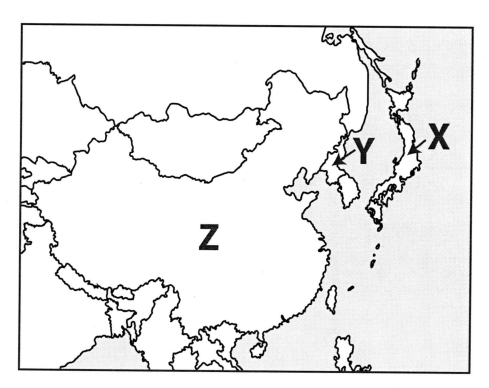

4. David wants to move to Eastern Asia to start a business. He wants to live in country that is economically strong, democratic, and has free markets. Which nation on the map above should David move to?

   A. X

   B. Y

   C. Z

   D. None of the countries above are both economically strong and democratic.

9.2 THE IMPACT OF SOUTHERN AND EASTERN ASIA ON INTERNATIONAL TRADE

PRODUCTS AND TRADE

Indian Textiles

Japanese Cars

Southern and Eastern Asia have great impact on world trade. For decades, Japan has produced some of the world's most popular products: computers, video games, cars, televisions, toys, electronic devices, and so on. Since opening their markets to world trade and competition, nations like China and India have also become major players. These nations produce textiles, processed foods, and various manufactured goods. Thanks to modern telecommunications (telephones and the Internet, for example) that allow people to communicate anywhere in the world, a number of U.S. service industries are starting to rely on employees in Southern and Eastern Asia to help meet customers' needs. Southern and Eastern Asian nations often produce products faster and cheaper than Western nations. Therefore, their products can be more affordable, creating consumer demand.

TRADE BARRIERS

In chapters three and six, we discussed **trade barriers**. Trade barriers are anything, either human-made or natural, that interfere with trade, such as tariffs, sanctions, embargoes, and natural barriers. As the world continues to globalize (become more connected), more and more trade barriers are falling.

Chinese Products

For nations in Southern and Eastern Asia, the removal of trade barriers can have good and bad consequences. When Western nations end tariffs, this helps Asian exports because it removes taxes. Since there are no taxes on Asian products, Asian producers can charge a lower price. This makes more people want to buy their products.

However, trade barriers can be useful for Asian nations seeking to protect their own markets. Tariffs on foreign products make these products cost more. This makes people in Asian nations want to buy products made at home. Without restrictions on foreign trade, less-developed nations sometimes have a hard time catching up to more-developed economies.

FACTORS OF ECONOMIC GROWTH

In chapters 3 and 6, we learned about the factors that influence economic growth in Africa and Southwest Asia. These factors include investments in human capital, capital goods, available natural resources, and the contributions of entrepreneurs. These same factors also impact the GDP of nations in Southern and Eastern Asia.

Developing economies like India's rely on international help to invest in human capital and capital goods. Foreign countries also provide aid in capital growth. Some of this help comes in the form of international donations. Much of it comes as foreign loans. The **World Bank** (international organization devoted to giving financial help to developing nations) provides much of this help. Projects financed by the World Bank have included investments in water sanitation, power output, and public services.

World Bank

China has made huge investments in human capital and capital goods over the last twenty years. The nation has introduced social programs that have helped some citizens escape poverty. Health care continues to improve as well. Meanwhile, the nation produces large amounts of capital goods. These goods continue to boost production and make China competitive on the world market.

Poverty (people living at an extremely low standard of living) is a huge enemy of economic growth. Poverty often means less education. This makes for a less-skilled workforce and slows development. Nations with high rates of poverty face the challenge of trying to produce enough revenue to help ease the suffering, while lacking much of the human capital they need to produce the needed growth. Overcoming poverty and sustaining economic growth will remain major challenges for much of Southern and Eastern Asia in years to come.

Poverty in Southern and Eastern Asia

Practice 9.2: The Impact of Southern and Eastern Asia on International Trade

1. How can tariffs hurt Southern and Eastern Asian economies?

2. How can tariffs help Southern and Eastern Asian economies?

3. How does the World Bank help developing economies in Southern and Eastern Asia?

4. How can poverty make it difficult for nations in Southern and Eastern Asia to develop economically?

CHAPTER 9 REVIEW

Key Terms

India's government
China's government
one-party system
China's Communist Party
Japan's government
constitutional monarchy
Diet
India's economy

China's economy
Japan's economy
North Korea's economy
South Korea's economy
trade barriers
World Bank
poverty

Chapter Review Questions

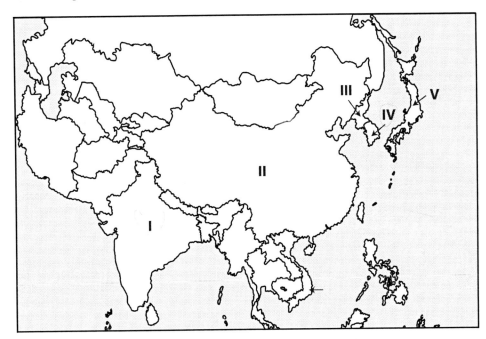

1. Which of the nations on the map above are **best** described as wealthy, developed economies?

   A. I and II   B. III and IV   C. II and V   D. IV and V

2. Which of the nations on the map above are **best** described as communist states?

   A. I and IV   B. II and III   C. II and V   D. I and IV

3. Which of the nations on the map above are **best** described as free democracies?

   A. IV and V   B. I and II   C. II and III   D. III and IV

4. The United States decides to raise tariffs on products from South Korea. This action will

   A. help South Korean producers.

   B. hurt South Korean producers.

   C. have no effect on South Korean producers.

   D. make South Korean products more competitive.

5. The Indian government wants India's consumers to buy products made at home. What is one thing the government could do to encourage consumers to buy Indian products?

   A. raise tariffs

   B. lower tariffs

   C. allow greater market competition

   D. lower the GDP

6. North Korea tests a nuclear missile. In response, many nations restrict trade with North Korea until it promises to stop making nuclear missiles. Such action is an example of

   A. tariffs.

   B. poverty.

   C. sanctions.

   D. capitalism.

7. Which nation has an emperor?

   A. Japan

   B. China

   C. India

   D. North Korea

8. Which nation suffers from severe poverty due to its command economy and communist state?

   A. South Korea

   B. India

   C. North Korea

   D. Japan

Chapter 10
Personal Money Management Choices

This chapter covers the following Georgia standard.

SS7E4	The student will explain personal money management choices in terms of income, spending, credit, saving, and investing.

INCOME AND SPENDING

Regardless of what part of the world people live in, they must make smart **personal moneymanagement choices**. They must handle their own money wisely.

Having a **budget** is an important part of having a wise money-management plan. A budget is a record of how you plan to spend your money. People who spend too much money fall into debt. **Debt** is the amount of money that you owe. People get in debt when they spend more money than they have and are forced to borrow.

Teenagers Shopping

INCOME

The first step to having an effective budget is to know your **income**. Income is how much money you have. For most people, their income is the amount of money they are paid by their employer. If they are self-employed, it is the money they make through their own business. A regular allowance from your parents is also a form of income.

Since employers usually pay workers every two weeks or once a month, most people operate on a weekly or monthly budget. It is important to know your income first, so that you know how much money you have to spend.

EXPENSES

Handwritten Budget

Credit Cards

Once you know your income, the second step is to know your **expenses**. Expenses are the things you spend money on. Some expenses require money every month. Buying groceries, paying your electric bill, and making a monthly house payment are all monthly expenses. Other expenses might only be temporary. Paying to get your television fixed or to cover a trip to the dentist might require money this month, but not the next. Others are flexible expenses. How much to spend on eating out or on clothes are examples of flexible expenses. You have freedom to decide how much money, if any, to spend. When you know your income and expenses, you can then decide how much money to spend. The key is to make sure that expenses are less than income.

Once you have a budget that works, you then need financial discipline to stick to it. Spend only what your budget allows because you know you can afford it. When people don't stick to a budget, they run the risk of getting into financial danger.

CREDIT

Sometimes debt is not bad. High-cost items like houses and cars could rarely be afforded without borrowed money. **Credit** is when you borrow someone else's money with an agreement to pay it back a little over time. Usually, you have to pay an **interest rate**. The interest rate is a percentage of the amount you owe. You agree to pay it *in addition* to what you borrowed. It is money you pay the lender in exchange for the use of their money to make a purchase.

For example, if you bought a $1000 television set using a credit card that charges 10 percent interest, you would actually pay $1100. Why? Because $100 is 10 percent of $1000, and $100 + $1000 = $1100. You paid the credit card company the extra $100 for the privilege of using their $1000 to get the television. People use credit cards for convenience, or because they want to buy something they cannot afford to pay for all at once. However, it is important to remember that the longer it takes you to pay off a credit card, the more money you spend on interest.

Unfortunately, because people often use credit cards to buy things they can't afford, U.S. citizens are falling deeper and deeper into debt. Failure to pay your debts can seriously damage your **credit score**. Your credit score is a number based on your history as a borrower. If you have a history of paying off loans and making monthly credit payments on time, then you will have a high credit score. If you are normally late with payments or have defaulted (failed to pay back loans), you will have a low credit score. Lenders use your credit score when deciding whether or not to loan you money and what interest rate to charge you. If you have a high credit score, then lenders are more likely to loan you money at a lower interest rate. If you have a low credit score, then your interest rate will be higher. If your score is low enough, you likely won't

Purchasing with Credit

get a loan at all. It is very important that citizens prove trustworthy and pay back any money they owe on time. Otherwise, they run the risk of not being able to borrow in the future.

SAVING AND INVESTING

Most U.S. citizens spend more money than they save. People get into debt when what they spend is greater than the amount of money they can afford to pay.

Spending is when you give money to someone or something in return for a good or service. You spend money to buy a video game, go to Six Flags, purchase new clothes, and so on.

Saving is when you take money you *could spend* and, instead, put it aside for a later time. Many people save by putting money in **savings accounts**. These are accounts people have with banks, credit unions, or even on-line institutions. They allow

Bank

people to save money, while having access to their money any time they want it.

Savings accounts also allow a person's money to gain interest. Remember, interest is the amount a borrower pays a lender for the use of their money. When you put your money in a savings account, you are actually lending it to that bank or institution in return for interest. The bank or credit union then uses your money to finance loans, make investments, and so on. Later, you can withdraw the money and interest. In most cases, the interest rate you earn on savings accounts is very little. Therefore, many citizens choose to save in other ways as well.

Investing is one of the most popular ways people save money. Investing is when you allow businesses to use part of your money in return for interest or a share of their profits (the money the business makes). The better the business does, the more money you make on your investment. It could be your own business that you invest in. Often, however, it is other peoples' businesses.

Wall Street

People invest in many ways. Many buy stocks, which make them part owner of a company. Others buy bonds, which does not give them ownership, but allows them to lend money to a business or institution. Many participate in mutual funds, which are made up of many companies so that, if one company does poorly, investors still make money off of those that are doing well. Still others might invest in CDs (certificates of deposit), which keep their money in a special account for a set period of time. Such forms of investment are popular because they tend to pay investors much more interest than simple savings accounts. However, they also offer investors less access to their money and require greater financial risk.

REASONS TO SAVE

Students in College

There are lots of reasons why people save. Sometimes, they save for a specific item they want to buy. Young couples often save to buy their first home, teenagers often save to buy a car, parents usually save to pay for their kids' college educations, and families might save to take a nice vacation.

One of the most important things citizens save for is retirement. When a person "retires," it means that they no longer work. People may retire due to an illness, or because they simply don't want to work anymore. The most common reason people retire is age.

However, even retired people still need money to live on. If they are not working and earning a salary (money paid by an employer), then this money must come from somewhere else. For many, it comes from retirement savings. Many people participate in 401(k) or pension plans through their employers. Others set up IRAs (individual retirement accounts).

Vacation

Retirement

CHAPTER 10 REVIEW

Key Terms and Concepts

personal moneymanagement choices
budget
debt
income
expenses
credit
interest rate

credit score
spending
saving
savings accounts
investing
reasons to save

Chapter 10 Review Questions

1. The ways you choose to save or spend money are your
   A. personal moneymanagement choices.
   B. income.
   C. savings.
   D. investments.

2. If you hope to borrow money in the future it is important to keep
   A. a low credit score.
   B. a high credit score.
   C. no credit score.
   D. plenty of debt.

3. In order for a budget to work well, it is important that
   A. you have debt.
   B. you have a high credit score.
   C. you invest.
   D. you keep your expenses less than your income.

4. Retirement, college, vacations, and a new wedding dress are all
   A. debts.
   B. things bought on credit.
   C. reasons to save.
   D. things people should not buy.

5. Look at the budget below. What will happen if Bill buys a car that will cost him $400.00 per month in car payments?

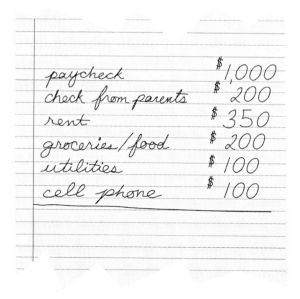

paycheck $1,000
check from parents $ 200
rent $ 350
groceries/food $ 200
utilities $ 100
cell phone $ 100

A. He will have less than $50 left over for any other expenses.

B. He will automatically go into debt.

C. His credit score will rise.

D. He will have to use his savings to pay for the car.

Georgia CRCT in SS: Africa and Asia Practice Test 1

The purpose of this practice test is to measure your progress in social studies. This test is based on the GPS-based Georgia CRCT in Social Studies and adheres to the sample question format provided by the Georgia Department of Education.

General Directions:

1. Read all directions carefully.

2. Read each question or sample. Then, choose the best answer.

3. Choose only one answer for each question. If you change an answer, be sure to erase your original answer completely.

1. Which of the following tends to increase a nation's GDP? SS7E3 SS7E7 SS7E10 CH 3, 6, 9

   A famine

   B poverty

   C investments in capital

   D limited natural resources

Read the quote below ,and answer the following question.

> "This nation has elements of both a parliamentary and presidential democracy."

2. Which nation could this quote be referring to? SS7CG1 SS7CG2 CH 3

   A Sudan

   B Saudi Arabia

   C South Africa

   D China

3. Many Southwest Asian nations are members of OPEC because the organization SS7E6 CH 6

   A combats AIDS in Africa.

   B provides famine relief.

   C controls oil exports.

   D promotes desalinization.

4. India is a republic. Its national government shares power with twenty-eight state governments. India is a/an SS7CG7 CH 9

   A autocracy.

   B federation.

   C unitary government.

   D confederation.

5. Why do desert regions in Southwest Asia have to import agricultural products? SS7G7 SS7E6 SS7E7 CH 4, 6

   A It increases revenue.

   B The governments of these regions would rather produce oil even though they could profit from agriculture.

   C They lack water and fertile soil.

   D They are too isolated to get heavy farm machinery in the region.

6. What is the best way to describe the role of Japan's emperor? SS7CG6 SS7CG7 CH 9

   A He is a dictator who rules the country.

   B He has no real power, but rather serves as a representative of the country.

   C He is elected by the people, and his decisions must be approved by parliament.

   D Japan has not had an emperor since World War II.

Look at the map below, and answer the question.

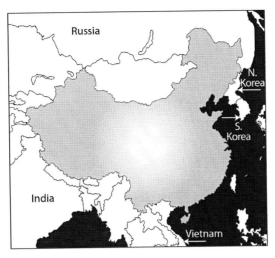

7. What form of government does the nation shaded in gray above have?   SS7CG1
   SS7H3
   CH 3. 6. 9

   A oligarchic

   B parliamentary democracy

   C constitutional monarchy

   D presidential democracy

8. Who decides what to produce in a command economy?   SS7E1
   SS7E5
   SS7E8
   CH 3, 6, 9

   A consumers

   B private business owners

   C the market

   D the state

9. Which of the following nations has had a market economy the longest?   SS7H3
   SS7E8
   CH 8, 9

   A Japan

   B China

   C India

   D North Korea

10. Which of the following left millions of Chinese citizens starving to death and living in failed communes?   SS7H3
    CH 8

    A the Long March

    B the Cultural Revolution

    C the Korean War

    D the Great Leap Forward

11. What are people called who start and own private businesses?   SS7E3
    SS7E7
    SS7E10
    CH 3, 6, 9

    A salesmen

    B investors

    C entrepreneurs

    D government spenders

Read the list below, and answer the following question.

- restrictions on pollution
- establishing parks and preserves
- declaring certain animals endangered

12. The **best** title for the list above is SS7G2
CH 1

    A Efforts to Protect Children

    B Attempts to Limit Families

    C Government Actions to Deal with Environmental Issues

    D Laws Enacted to Protect Citizens' Rights

13. A less-skilled workforce and lower literacy rates are both causes of SS7E4
SS7G8
SS7G12
CH 1, 4, 7

    A market economies.

    B democracy.

    C capitalism.

    D poverty.

14. Why are Israel's politics influenced by religion? SS7H2
SS7CG5
CH 5, 6

    A It was founded as a Jewish homeland.

    B It is an Islamic republic.

    C Devout Muslims create Israel's policies.

    D The Qur'an has strong influence.

15. The Tigris, Euphrates, and Nile rivers help farmers by providing a source of SS7G2
SS7G6
CH 1, 4

    A desalinization.   C irrigation.

    B flooding.   D pollution.

16. Water pollution is a major concern in Southwest Asia because in many regions SS7G6
CH 4

    A most of the land is covered by water.

    B flooding is common year round.

    C water is scarce.

    D Buddhism is the dominant religion.

17. You need a personal budget to SS7E4
CH 10

    A get more credit cards.

    B invest intelligently.

    C vote in political races.

    D make good money choices.

18. Why do **most** people of Southwest Asia live close to water supplies? SS7G7
CH 4

    A Most of Southwest Asia is dry and water is incredibly important.

    B They rely on rivers for bathing and cleaning.

    C They enjoy swimming and fishing as hobbies.

    D Rivers and seas provide safety from foreign invasion.

Look at the map below, and answer the following question.

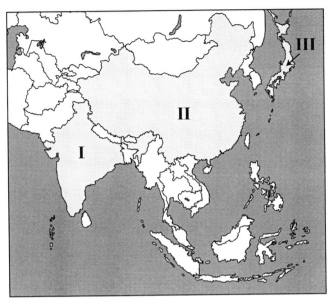

19. In which of these areas would one **most likely** find people who practice Confucianism and Buddhism, even though it is technically an atheist country? SS7G9 SS7G12 CH 7

   A I

   B II

   C III

   D None

20. Why are people who live in the savannas typically less nomadic than those in the Sahel or Sahara? SS7G1 SS7G3 CH 1

   A Water is more abundant.

   B Their homes are permanent shelters made out of mud and rocks.

   C They are sheep herders.

   D They do not need to hunt wildlife for food.

21. **Most** Arabs in Southwest Asia dislike Israel because SS7H2 CH 5

   A Israel is a Persian nation.

   B the United Nations gave Israeli Jews land that Palestinian Arabs believe belongs to them.

   C Israelis export more oil than any other country and is the wealthiest nation in Southwest Asia.

   D Israel is a strong ally of most Muslim nations.

Look at the map below, and answer the following question.

22. The nation shaded in the map above is **best** described as a/an

SS7CG1
SS7CG2
CH 3

    A democratic confederation.

    B Jewish hierocracy.

    C unitary autocracy.

    D traditional tribal unit.

23. Bantu, Swahili, and Ashanti peoples live in various parts of

SS7G4
CH 1

    A Africa.

    B Southwest Asia.

    C Eastern Asia.

    D Southern Asia.

24. Which of the following geographic features is located in southern Africa?

SS7G1
CH 1

    A Sahara Desert

    B Gobi Desert

    C Kalahari Desert

    D Strait of Hormuz

25. What is the **major** reason for the conflicts between Israel and the Arab world?

SS7H2
CH 5

    A Arabs support Jewish nationalism.

    B Israelis believe Palestinians should have part of Palestine.

    C Arabs claim Palestine is theirs.

    D Arabs and Israelis both claim the Strait of Hormuz.

Read the list below, and answer the following question.

1. They brought advanced forms of agriculture and iron tools to southern Africa.

2. They transformed southern Africa into a farming and herding society.

3. They transformed southern Africa into a hunting-gathering society.

4. They were one of the largest population movements in history.

5. Today, they only make up a small portion of South Africa's population.

26. Choose the above statements that are accurate in describing the Bantu people. SS7G4 CH 1

   A 1, 3, 5   C 1, 3, 4

   B 2, 3, 5   D 1, 2, 4

27. The United States and other nations imposed sanctions against Iran to protest its nuclear energy program. What is this an example of? SS7E2 SS7E6 SS7E9 CH 3, 6, 9

   A political trade barrier

   B desertification

   C natural trade barrier

   D exchange rate

28. Which of the following countries pursued capitalism and democracy after independence? SS7H1 SS7CG2 CH 2, 3

   A North Korea

   B Saudi Arabia

   C China

   D Kenya

29. Turkey has a developing economy that encourages private ownership of property and business. Meanwhile, the government still regulates banks and various other industries. Turkey's economy is **best** described as a SS7E5 CH 6

   A traditional economy.

   B mixed economy.

   C command economy.

   D market economy.

30. During the 1950s, several nations went to war in an effort to control a human-made waterway connecting the Mediterranean Sea to the Red Sea. What geographic feature did these nations want to control? SS7G5 CH 4

   A Nile River

   B Strait of Hormuz

   C Persian Gulf

   D Suez Canal

31. Which of the following rivers runs through India? SS7G9 CH 7

   A Mekong   C Indus

   B Euphrates   D Nile

32. What is one challenge facing Nigeria's economy? SS7E3 CH 3

   A It is overdeveloped.

   B It has too many foreign investors.

   C It is overdependent on its oil reserves for national income.

   D It is a command economy and the government enforces strict laws.

Look at the map below, and answer the following question.

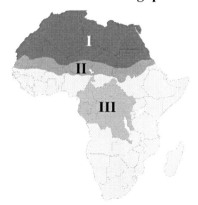

33. Which region is home to the rainforests?

SS7G1
CH 1

   A I   B II   C I and II   D III

34. When did the Ottoman Empire finally come to an end?

SS7H2
CH 5

  A immediately after the Balkan Wars of 1912

  B during the rule of Sultan Abdulhamid II

  C after World War I

  D during rapid growth of European powers in 1908

35. Who are entrepreneurs?

SS7E4
CH 10

  A investors in education and training

  B investors in new technology

  C people who start and own private businesses

  D people who refuse to participate in economic growth

36. In which area would one expect to find the most wealth and the lowest amount of poverty?

SS7G3
SS7G7
SS7G11
SS7E3
SS7E7
SS7E10
CH 1, 4, 7
CH 3, 6, 9

  A rural China

  B Tokyo, Japan

  C North Korea

  D rural Africa

37. Israel is led by a prime minister. The prime minister is the leader of whichever party holds a majority of seats in the Knesset. Israel is a

SS7CG4
CH 6

  A parliamentary democracy.

  B presidential democracy.

  C command economy.

  D Jewish oligarchy.

38. Political instability in Africa has contributed to

SS7CG3
CH 3

  A the rapid spread of AIDS.

  B fewer civil wars.

  C less refugees.

  D fast relief for people suffering from the effects of famines.

39. North and South Korea are divided **mainly** over

SS7H3
SS7CG6
SS7H3
CH 8, 9

  A religious differences.

  B political differences.

  C trade barriers.

  D desertification.

40. Which two of the following African nations are democratic?

SS7CG1
SS7CG2
CH 3

    I. India

    II. Kenya

    III. Sudan

    IV. South Africa

A I and IV   C II and III

B II and IV   D I and II

41. Civil wars contribute to starvation, poverty, and the spread of AIDS in Africa because they

SS7CG3
CH 3

A establish democracies.

B interfere with desertification.

C make it difficult for suffering people to get relief.

D cause air pollution.

42. What is the importance of oil to the Southwest Asia?

SS7E6
SS7E7
CH 6

A Oil is not the major export of the Southwest Asia, so it is only slightly significant to the overall growth or decline of their economy.

B Oil encourages conflict-free trading with other nations.

C Oil makes the region strategically important, maintains the region's economy, and gives Southwest Asian nations international influence.

D Oil makes the region an area of little importance.

43. In which of the following ways is Saudi Arabia different from Iran?

SS7CG5
CH 6

A Saudi Arabia is a theocracy, but Iran is a monarchy.

B Iran is a theocracy, but Saudi Arabia is a monarchy.

C Most people in Saudi Arabia are Muslims, while most people in Iran are Hindus.

D Most Saudis are Persians, while most Iranians are Jewish Arabs.

44. Countries sometimes allow only limited trade with a certain country in order to force it to change a specific policy. What is this called?

SS7E2
SS7E6
SS7E9
CH 3, 6, 9

A tariffs   C sanctions

B embargoes   D blocks

45. Which religion did **not** originate in Southwest Asia?

SS7H2
SS7G8
SS7G12
CH 3, 4, 7

A Buddhism

B Christianity

C Judaism

D Islam

46. What type of government is Iran?

SS7CG5
CH 6

A a communist state

B a constitutional monarchy

C an Islamic republic

D a democratic republic

47. Which nation is a constitutional monarchy?

SS7G9
SS7CG1
SS7CG7
CH 3, 7, 9

A Japan   C China

B Kenya   D Afghanistan

Look at the map below, and answer the following question.

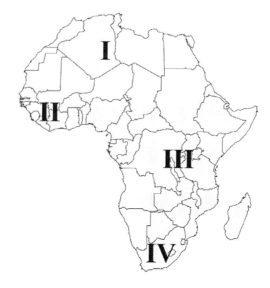

48. Someone traveling directly from Egypt to the southernmost part of Africa would travel through which regions?

SS7G1
CH 1

A   I and II   B   II and III   C   I only   D   III and IV

Look at the list below and answer the following question.

The Ghanaian independence movement	Kwame Nkrumah
India's independence movement	Mohandas Gandhi
South Africa's anti-apartheid movement	X
Chinese Revolution	Mao Zedong

49. What name should go where you see the 'X'?

SS7H1
CH 2

A   Ho Chi Minh   C   Patrice Lumumba

B   Nelson Mandela   D   Saddam Hussein

50. Which of the following can cause health problems in parts of China?

SS7G10
CH 4

A   air pollution in Cairo

B   AIDS in sub-Saharan countries

C   pollution in the Yangtze River

D   pollution in the Nile River

51. Which of the following areas tends to have the largest populations in Africa, Southwest Asia, and Southern/Eastern Asia?

SS7G3
SS7G7
SS7G11
CH 1, 4, 7

A   mountain regions

B   rural communities

C   cities

D   deserts

Look at the map below, and answer the following question.

52. The dominant religion in the shaded country on in the map is

   A   Christianity.   B   Islam.   C   Judaism.   D   Buddhism.

Look at the map below and answer the following question.

53. The shaded area depicts

   A   the Sahara Desert.   C   the Kalahari Desert.

   B   African Rainforests.   D   the Himalayas.

54. Traditionally, how much access have women in Sudan had to education? SS7CG3 CH 3

   A They have traditionally received more education than men.

   B Sudanese women have traditionally had less access to education than men.

   C Women have never been educated in Sudan.

   D Sudan does not offer any education to its citizens.

55. Which of the following two countries lean the **most** towards command economies? SS7E1 SS7E8 CH 3, 9

   A China and Japan

   B China and North Korea

   C India and Israel

   D Kenya and South Korea

56. Jeremy's company has asked him to analyze its new factory in Kenya. Jeremy recommends that the company buy more machines and hire more workers for the factory. What economic question is Jeremy trying to answer? SS7E1 SS7E5 SS7E8 CH 3, 6, 9

   A what to produce

   B for whom to produce

   C how to produce

   D where to sell

57. China's economy is SS7E1 SS7E8 CH 3, 6

   A a mixed economy.

   B too dependent on oil.

   C the wealthiest in Africa.

   D a strictly command economy.

58. Mao Zedong and Ho Chi Minh were both SS7H3 CH 8

   A great emperors of China.

   B leaders of Japan during WWII.

   C promoters of the Great Leap Forward.

   D nationalist leaders in southeast Africa.

59. In many African and Asian communities, people make a living in the same way that their parents and ancestors always have. They want to produce enough to survive but often aren't concerned with mass economic development. These communities operate as SS7E1 SS7E5 SS7E8 CH 3, 6, 9

   A command economies.

   B traditional economies.

   C market economies.

   D mixed economies that are mostly a command economies.

60. The ANC was **most** supportive of SS7H1 CH 2

   A apartheid.

   B colonialism.

   C Nelson Mandela.

   D Mao Zedong.

61. What country in Africa has benefited greatly from the availability of capital goods?

SS7E3 CH 3

A Nigeria

C Sudan

B Chad

D South Africa

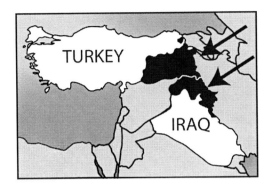

62. Which people group occupies the area on the map above?

SS7G4 SS7G8 SS7G12 CH 1, 4, 7

A Swahili

C Kurds

B Jews

D Hindus

63. The fact that Japan is a small island nation means that

SS7G11 SS7E8 SS7E9 CH 7, 9

A it depends on trade for survival.

B it still has an emperor.

C it has a market economy.

D Japanese people swim better than Americans.

64. Which of the following nations is part of Southern Asia?

SS7G5 CH 7

A Israel

B Kenya

C India

D Japan

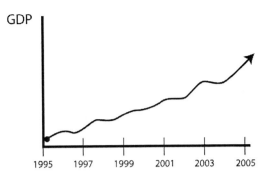

65. According to the chart above, what **most likely** occurred in India from 1995 to 2005?

SS7E3 SS7E7 SS7E10 CH 3, 6, 9

A India became a command economy.

B India invested more in capital goods and human capital.

C India's natural resources decreased.

D India stopped encouraging entrepreneurship.

66. Economic development is helped by

SS7E3 SS7E7 SS7E10 CH 3, 6, 9

A strict government control.

B low literacy rates.

C available natural resources.

D limits on artistic expression.

67. When you choose to use part of your money to buy stocks, bonds, or put it in some other kind of savings that pays interest, you are

SS7E4 CH 10

A spending.

B accumulating debt.

C investing.

D using credit.

Look at the map below, and answer the following question.

68. Which bodies of water are depicted in the shaded area? SS7G5
CH 4

   A Jordan River and Strait of Hormuz

   B Black Sea and Caspian Sea

   C Jordan River and Euphrates River

   D Tigris River and Euphrates River

Factors that increase GDP
Investments in human capital
Wise use of natural resources
Investments in capital
New technology
Foreign investments

69. Which of the following should go in the blank box above? SS7E3 SS7E7 SS7E10 CH 3, 6, 9

   A More entrepreneurship

   B Higher tariffs

   C More trade barriers

   D Less entrepreneurship

70. Which of the following areas remains divided into two opposing countries? SS7G9 SS7E8 CH 7, 9

   A. Korea Peninsula

   B. Vietnam

   C. Pakistan

   D. Indonesia

Georgia CRCT in SS: Africa and Asia Practice Test 2

The purpose of this practice test is to measure your progress in social studies. This test is based on the GPS-based Georgia CRCT in Social Studies and adheres to the sample question format provided by the Georgia Department of Education.

General Directions:

1. Read all directions carefully.

2. Read each question or sample. Then choose the best answer.

3. Choose only one answer for each question. If you change an answer, be sure to erase your original answer completely.

1. Nomadic people who live in desert regions often travel by   SS7G3 CH 1

    A. boat.

    B. train.

    C. camel.

    D. bicycle.

2. Which of the following nation's economy is determined by market demand?   SS7E1 SS7E5 SS7E8 CH 3, 6, 9

    A. China   C. Egypt

    B. North Korea   D. Japan

3. Which of the following makes it difficult for China to feed its 1.3 billion people?   SS7G9 SS7G11 SS7E3 SS7E7 SS7E10 CH 7, 9

    A. Only 10 percent of the land is suitable for agriculture.

    B. Families are only allowed to have one child.

    C. The government is allowing more market competition.

    D. Nations like the United States are buying more and more Chinese goods.

4. In what country does the government control almost all aspects of the economy?   SS7E5 CH 6

    A. Israel

    B. Japan

    C. Saudi Arabia

    D. Turkey

5. In which regions would one find the **most** Arab peoples?   SS7G4 SS7G8 CH 1, 4

    A. North Africa and Southwest Asia

    B. southern Africa and Iran

    C. China and India

    D. Vietnam and central Africa

6. Where would one expect the **most** people to live in Southern Asia?   SS7G11 CH 7

    A. the Himalayas

    B. Gobi Desert

    C. New Delhi, India

    D. Kenya

7. How does religion influence the government of Saudi Arabia?   SS7G8 SS7CG5 CH 4, 6

    A. The Holy Bible is used to create the policies and laws of the country.

    B. There is little religious influence found in the government.

    C. The Qur'an and other Muslim teachings provide the basis for its government and laws.

    D. Both Judaism and Christianity are used to establish laws and policies.

Look at the map below, and answer the following question.

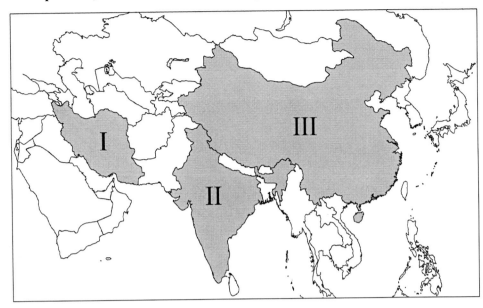

8. In which area would one expect to find a country that is **mostly** Muslim?

SS7G8
SS7G12
CH 4, 7

   A. I

   B. II

   C. III

   D. II and III

9. Someone who believed that all black Africans must see themselves as one people in order to gain independence and overcome the effects of European colonization would have been **most** supportive of

SS7H1
CH 2

   A. capitalism.

   B. Pan-Africanism.

   C. apartheid.

   D. Afrikaners.

10. Which of the following is a major environmental issue in Kenya?

SS7G2
CH 1

   A. desalinization

   B. illegal hunting of wildlife

   C. runaway capitalism

   D. an oppressive oligarchy

11. Kenya began offering free education in 2003. How has this affected the literacy rate in Kenya?   SS7CG3 CH 3

    A. It has helped the literacy rate.

    B. More Kenyans are illiterate than ever before.

    C. The literacy rate has not been affected because literacy has little to do with education.

    D. There is no literacy rate in Kenya.

12. Why does international trade involve an exchange rate of currency?   SS7E2 SS7E6 SS7E9 CH 3, 6, 9

    A. because countries use different forms of money

    B. because international trading is expensive and some countries have no money

    C. to ensure that all countries are increasing the value of their currency

    D. because Southwest Asia has laws that require foreign countries to trade at a lesser cost than the current rate of exchange

13. More industry, more capital goods, greater production, and large amounts of foreign investment in a nation are usually signs of   SS7E3 SS7E7 SS7E10 CH 3, 6, 9

    A. Pan-Africanism.

    B. command economies.

    C. economic development.

    D. apartheid.

14. In which of the following nations does a president exercise the **most** power?   SS7CG2 CH 3

    A. Israel

    B. Japan

    C. Kenya

    D. India

15. Why did Islam divide into two factions after AD 632?   SS7G8 CH 4

    A. Muhammad wanted to change the religious laws.

    B. Disagreements arose over leadership.

    C. The enemies of Muhammad finally conquered him.

    D. Disputes erupted over religious territories in Southwest Asia.

16. Israel is **best** described as a/an   SS7CG5 CH 6

    A. Islamic theocracy that exports oil.

    B. parliamentary democracy with a developed economy.

    C. presidential democracy ruled by Arabs.

    D. Jewish autocracy.

17. Which of the following is a **major** environmental issue in the shaded regions on the map above?

    A. desalinization

    B. deforestation

    C. available water

    D. AIDS

18. What type of government gives a dictator complete control?

    A. democracy

    B. republics

    C. autocracy

    D. command economies

19. What are embargoes and tariffs examples of?

    A. natural trade barriers

    B. natural resources

    C. political trade barriers

    D. capital goods

20. Human development and poor soil can often decrease the size of African rainforests. When rainforests decrease in size, it is called

SS7G2 CH 1

A. desertification.

B. deforestation.

C. desalinization.

D. famine.

21. Which of the following are major religions among Swahili peoples?

SS7G4 CH 1

A. Islam

B. traditional religions

C. neither A nor B

D. both A and B

22. Which of the following factors has helped Japan become the second-wealthiest nation in the world?

SS7E8 CH 9

A. its command economy

B. its market economy

C. trade isolation

D. state-owned industries

23. The **most common** religion in India is

A. Islam.

B. Hinduism.

C. Buddhism.

D. Christianity.

SS7G12 CH 7

24. When the United States and European nations decide to end tariffs on Indian textiles, India benefits from

SS7E2 SS7E6 SS7E9 CH 3, 6, 9

A. free trade.

B. trade barriers.

C. sanctions.

D. embargoes.

25. In which of the following countries do citizens play the **greatest** role in deciding who serves as their political leader?

SS7CG7 CH 9

A. China

B. Saudi Arabia

C. Japan

D. Sudan

26. South Africa's government **most** resembles a/an

SS7CG2 CH 3

A. autocratic dictatorship.

B. oligarchic command system.

C. confederation.

D. parliamentary democracy.

27. In which of the following forms of government do citizens have the **least** amount of power?

SS7CG1 SS7CG2 SS7CG4 SS7CG5 SS7CG6 SS7CG7 CH 3, 6, 9

A. parliamentary democracy

B. presidential democracy

C. constitutional monarchy

D. absolute monarchy

Use the map below to answer question 28.

28. The shaded region depicts which country?

SS7G5
CH 4

   A. Jordan   B. Israel   C. Saudi Arabia   D. Iraq

Use the map below to answer question 29.

29. The map above highlights the

SS7G1
CH 1

   A. Mekong River.   C. Nile River.

   B. Congo River.   D. Indus River.

Read the list below, and answer the following question.

- If Turkey builds a dam on the Tigris River, it affects Iraq as well.
- Israel and Jordan may have conflicts over the Jordan River.
- Bedouins and farmers feud over well rights.
- Growing cities put strain on limited water supplies.

30. What **major** concern among Southwest Asia countries do these examples represent? SS7G6 CH 4

    A. pollution

    B. scarcity of water

    C. abundance of water

    D. religious conflict

31. How do foreign investors help a country's economy? SS7E3 SS7E7 SS7E10 CH 3, 6, 9

    A. They bring money into the economy.

    B. They establish command economies.

    C. They establish a power struggle within the country.

    D. They produce high tariffs within the country.

32. Today, where do **most** Southwest Asians live? SS7G7 CH 4

    A. in the mountains

    B. in deserts

    C. in the savannas

    D. in cities

33. What happened in China in 1949 that impacted the cold war and concerned the United States? SS7H3 CH 8

    A. China's economy opened to free markets.

    B. China became a communist state.

    C. North Korea invaded South Korea.

    D. China became a parliamentary system.

34. North Korea's economy is **best** described as SS7H3 CH 8

    A. market and underdeveloped.

    B. mixed and developed.

    C. command and underdeveloped.

    D. democratic and wealthy.

35. By allowing market competition and private ownership, nations like India and Japan encourage people to become SS7E3 SS7E7 SS7E10 CH 3, 6, 9

    A. politicians.

    B. Communists.

    C. entrepreneurs.

    D. teachers.

36. If you spend more money than you have, then you will have SS7E4 CH 10

    A. debt.   C. a budget.

    B. credit.   D. savings.

Look at the map below, and answer the following question.

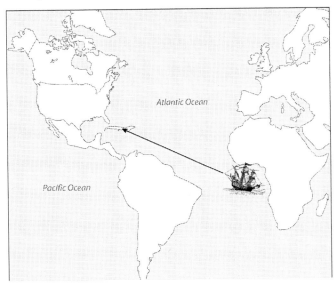

37. The map depicts

SS7H1
SS7E2
CH 2, 3

   A. trade between Africa and the North America.

   B. trade between the Western Hemisphere and the Ottoman Empire.

   C. trade between Egypt and Japan.

   D. voyages around South Africa.

38. What is a **major** concern of Southwest Asia in regard to industrialization?

SS7G6
CH 4

   A. It creates competition between the locals and the tourists.

   B. It decreases the value of the currency within the region.

   C. It causes the government to raise taxes.

   D. It creates pollutants that affect the quality of air and water.

39. Which of the following causes great problems for China?

SS7G10
CH 7

   A. market economies

   B. volcanic eruptions

   C. pollution

   D. Islamic terrorism

40. Punah lives in Southern Asia. He starts his own business. Punah is a/an

SS7E3
SS7E7
SS7E10
SS710
CH 3, 6, 9

   A. entrepreneur.

   B. trade barrier.

   C. investor in human capital.

   D. citizen in a command economy.

Use the map below to answer question 41.

41. Which of the following features could be accurately labeled in the shaded area?

    A. Gaza Strip

    B. Nile River

    C. Himalayan Mountains

    D. Tigris River

SS7G5
CH 4

Use the map below to answer question 42.

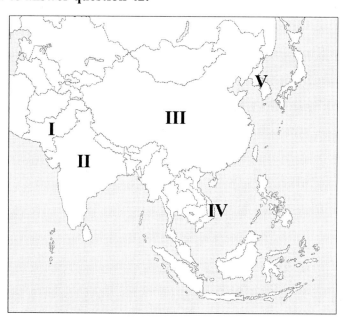

42. The Vietnam War was fought in which area?

    A. IV   B. V   C. I   D. II and III

SS7H3
CH 8

43. Following World War I, many Africans were disappointed to learn that they would not be granted their independence by European colonizers. This disappointment led to

SS7H1 CH 2

A. the Middle Passage.

B. the South African War.

C. the Berlin Conference.

D. African nationalist movements.

44. In which of the following forms of government do citizens have the **most** power?

SS7CG1 SS7CG2 SS7CG4 SS7CG5 SS7CG6 SS7CG7 CH 3, 6, 9

A. autocracies

B. oligarchies

C. monarchies

D. democracies

45. An African devoted to uniting all black Africans in an effort to improve economic and political stability across the continent would **most likely** want to be a member of

SS7H1 CH 2

A. the African Union.

B. Vietcong.

C. OPEC.

D. al Qaeda.

46. Certain taxes interfere with trade because they raise prices and make it less profitable for countries to sell their goods in foreign markets. What are these taxes called?

SS7E2 SS7E6 SS7E9 CH 3, 6, 9

A. embargoes

B. political barriers

C. international taxes

D. tariffs

47. Which country remains one of the few absolute monarchies in the world today?

SS7CG5 CH 6

A. Israel

B. Saudi Arabia

C. Iran

D. South Korea

48. Which of the following affects trade the **least**?

SS7E2 SS7E3 SS7E4 SS7E6 SS7E7 SS7E9 SS7E10 CH 3, 6, 9, 10

A. geographic location

B. natural resources

C. government policies

D. personal money-management decisions

49. What type of economy is found in Turkey?

SS7E5 CH 6

A. a free-market economy

B. a command economy

C. a market economy

D. a mixed economy

Look at the map below, and answer the following question.

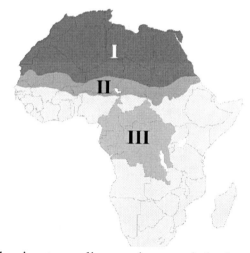

50. A tourist in Africa hoping to see lions, zebras, and elephants should visit which of the regions on the map?

SS7G1
CH 1

   A. II

   B. III

   C. I

   D. None of these regions would be home to these animals.

Read the statement below ,and answer the following question.

> "Jesus is the promised Messiah and the son of God. He was crucified by the Roman government, and he died to pay for humankind's sins. After three days, he arose and ascended to heaven. The only way to know God and find salvation is through faith in Jesus."

51. Which religion is this passage **most likely** describing?

SS7G8
CH 4

   A. Judaism

   B. Christianity

   C. Buddhism

   D. Islam

52. The effects of anti-Semitism, Zionism, and the Holocaust led to the creation of which modern state?

SS7H2
SS7G8
CH 5, 4

   A. Palestine

   B. Iran

   C. Lebanon

   D. Israel

53. The mountains of Afghanistan and the deserts on the Arabian Peninsula are examples of what?

SS7E2
SS7E6
SS7E9
CH 3, 6, 9

   A. natural resources

   B. natural trade barriers

   C. political trade barriers

   D. key imports

Look at the map below ,and answer the following question.

54. The shaded region depicts what country?

SS7G5
CH 4

   A. Jordan   B. Israel   C. Saudi Arabia   D. Iraq

55. Which of the following state-ments **best** describes Sudan's educational system?
SS7CG3
CH 3

   A. Boys tend to be more educated than girls.

   B. Children are not allowed to attend schools because they are needed to help farm.

   C. Girls go to school, while boys join the military or work.

   D. Sudan has more college graduates than any other African nation.

56. In which of the following nations do citizens have the **least** amount of power?
SS7CG7
CH 9

   A. Israel

   B. Turkey

   C. Japan

   D. China

57. The necessity to meet the needs of its massive population has led China to
SS7E8
CH 9

   A. allow more free-market competition.

   B. place strict controls on literacy.

   C. invade neighboring countries.

   D. allow more than one party to help run the government.

58. By moving away from a command economy, India has benefited from
SS7E8
CH 9

   A. state-owned industries.

   B. government regulations.

   C. trade isolation.

   D. foreign investments.

Look at the map below, and answer question 59.

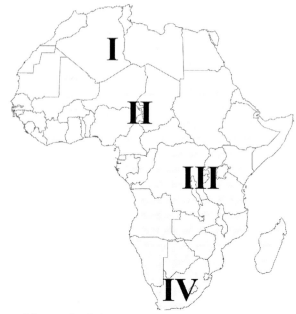

59. In which region would one find the ANC?

SS7H1
CH 2

    A. I   B. II   C. III   D. IV

Look at the map below, and answer question 60.

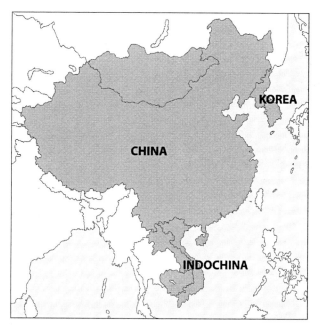

60. Which of the following can be found in the shaded area?

SS7G9
CH 7

    A. Muhammad's birthplace   C. Tokyo

    B. the Himalayas   D. the Indus Valley

61. What physical feature in Sudan contributes to crop production and fertile land?
SS7G1 CH 1

A. the Nile River

B. the Atlas Mountains

C. the Suez Canal

D. the Congo River

62. According to the graph below, what **most likely** happened in the early 1970s?
SS7E6 CH 6

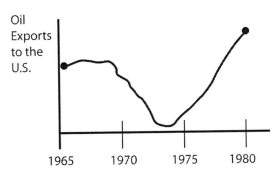

Oil Exports to the U.S.

1965   1970   1975   1980

A. African nations raised U.S. tariffs.

B. OPEC declared an oil embargo against the United States.

C. Israel stopped exporting oil.

D. China became a communist state.

63. Many nations in Africa, Southwest Asia, Southern Asia, and Eastern Asia are attempting to improve their economies by providing better health care and education for their citizens. Improving health care and education are examples of investing in
SS7E3 SS7E7 SS7E10 CH 3, 6, 9

A. capital.

B. human capital.

C. natural resources.

D. entrepreneurship.

64. In which region would one **most likely** find cattle herders who are not nomadic?
SS7G3 CH 1

A. African savanna

B. Sahara Desert

C. East Jerusalem

D. African rainforests

65. People who depend on the Yangtze are **most** impacted by
SS7G10 CH 7

A. deforestation.

B. desertification.

C. AIDS.

D. water pollution.

66. Gobin is Ashanti. He follows traditional Ashanti religious beliefs, but some of his Ashanti friends have converted to Christianity or Islam. Which of the following statements is **true**?
SS7G4 CH 1

A. Gobin's friends are not really Christians or Muslims because they are Ashanti.

B. Ashanti is Gobin's ethnic group.

C. Traditional religions define Gobin's ethnic group.

D. Ashanti cannot become a Buddhist.

67. What event occurred in 1948 that caused conflict in Southwest Asia that continues today?
SS7H2 CH 5

A. Saudi Arabia became a monarchy.

B. Iran became an Islamic theocracy.

C. The modern state of Israel was founded.

D. The United States invaded Iraq.

68. Which of the following demon- SS7H1
strated Europeans' lack of con- CH 2
cern for black Africans during
the nineteenth century?

A. Pan-Africanism

B. African socialism

C. the Berlin Conference

D. apartheid

69. The **longest** river in the world SS7G1
is the CH 1

A. Euphrates.

B. Tigris.

C. Nile.

D. Amazon.

Look at the map below, and answer the following question.

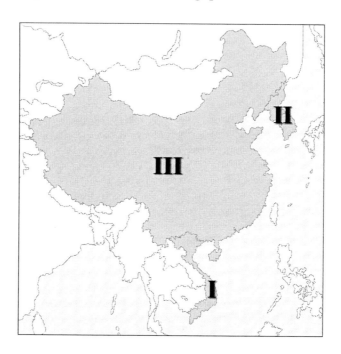

70. Ho Chi Minh led a nationalist movement in the country labeled SS7G9
SS7H3
CH 7, 8

A I.   B II.   C III.   D none of these

174